Points of Issue

A Compendium of Points of Issue of Books by 19th-20th Century Authors

Compiled by Bill McBride

Copyright, 1996, by William M. McBride and his heirs, Emily Anne and Ross Evans McBride.

Third edition, 5th printing.

ISBN # 0-930313-04-6

A Publication of
McBride/Publisher
56 Arbor Street
Hartford CT 06106

To order or inquire about this or other publications, please call 860-523-1622 between 9 AM and 6 PM, Eastern time, daily.
Or visit our website at:
www.mcbridepublisher.com
or reach us by email at
bill@jumpingfrog.com

Copies available at $12.95 plus $1.00 postage & handling by 1st class mail. Single copies are full-price to all. Five or more copies: 40% off, plus shipping.

Single copies of the companion to this book, **A Pocket Guide to the Identification of First Editions**, Sixth Edition (2000), are available for $12.95 plus $1.00 shipping & handling, 1st Class Mail. Same discounts apply to multiple copy purchases of five or more.

Printed & bound by
Budget Printing, Hartford, Connecticut

Wouk, Herman. Aurora Dawn. NY, 1947.
    CP: *Manufactured in the United States of America by American Book-Stratford Press, Inc., New York.*
    BC: no Book club deboss at bottom near spine
Wright, Richard. Black Boy. NY, (1945). DJ: front flap: *$2.50* and *No. 5760* ; back flap: *No. 5761* ; back panel: *No. 2209*
Wright, Richard. Native Son. NY, 1940. B: blue cloth   FC & CP: title in red and light blue blocks   DJ: yellow & green
Wylie, Elinor Hoyt. Jennifer Lorn. NY, 1923.
    TP: integral, line 5 *tegmine,* line 9 *Poyngard*
Wylie, Elinor Hoyt. Nets to Catch the Wind. NY, 1921.
    PA: unwatermarked   SP: stamped, no label
Wylie, Elinor Hoyt. The Orphan Angel. NY, 1926.
    CP: copyright   339: colophon has 13 lines
Wylie, Elinor Hoyt. Trivial Breath. NY, 1928. 13.9: *In*
Wylie, Elinor Hoyt. The Venetian Glass Nephew. NY, 1925.
    CP: no usual George H. Doran *GHD* monogram
Yeats, William Butler. The Celtic Twilight. L, 1893.
    SP: *LAWRENCE AND BULLEN*
Young, Stark. So Red the Rose. NY, 1934.
    P.1 of text: no list of characters facing

Wodehouse, P.G. Biffens Millions. NY, 1964. SP: *P.J. Wodehouse*
Wodehouse, P.G. Carry On, Jeeves. L, 1925.
    Verso of HT: 13 titles ending with *The Coming of Bill*
Wodehouse, P.G. The Clicking of Cuthbert. L, 1922.
    Verso of HT: eight titles ending with *The Girl on the Boat*
Wodehouse, P.G. The Girl on the Boat. L, 1922. Verso of HT: eight titles ending with *The Clicking of Cuthbert*
Wodehouse, P.G. The Heart of a Goof. L, 1926.
    Verso of HT: 14 titles ending with *The Coming of Bill*
Wodehouse, P.G. Indiscretions of Archie. L, 1921.
    Verso of HT: six titles ending with *Jill the Reckless* 31.12: *friend potatoes*
Wodehouse, P.G. The Inimitable Jeeves. L, 1923. Verso of HT: ten titles ending with *The Clicking of Cuthbert*
Wodehouse, P.G. Jeeves in the Offing. L, (1960).
    HT: *A Few Quick Ones*
Wodehouse, P.G. Leave it to Psmith. L, 1924. Verso of HT: eleven titles ending with *Love Among the Chickens*
Wodehouse, P.G. The Little Nugget. NY, (1914).
    CP: *Published January*
Wodehouse, P.G. Louder and Funnier. L, (1932).
    B: yellow cloth
Wodehouse, P.G. Money in the Bank. L,(1946). B: orange cloth
Wodehouse, P.G. The Pothunters. L, 1902. ADS: none
Wodehouse, P.G. Right Ho, Jeeves. L, 1934.
    CP: lacks usual First Printing notice
Wodehouse, P.G. Ukridge. L, 1924.
    Verso of HT: thirteen titles ending with *Leave it to Psmith*
Wodehouse, P.G. William Tell Told Again. L, 1904. ADS: 2 pp.
Wolfe, Thomas. From Death To Morning. NY, 1935.
    B: brown V cloth   ST: gilt in blindstamped panels
Wolfe, Thomas. Look Homeward, Angel. NY, 1929.
    DJ: author's portrait   CP: Scribner's seal
Woolf, Leonard. Barbarians at the Gate. L, 1939.
    B: pink paper over boards
Woolf, Virginia. On Being III. (L), 1930. 5: rule through *125* with *250* inserted above and marked out of series

About this Guide.

Points of Issue lists points in books by authors of the 19th and 20th centuries. Information for this guide was obtained from dealer catalogs, bibliographies and other source material variously available. In addition, new points of issue, much concerning dustjackets, appears here for the first time.

    This guide is not intended to be exhaustive of all collected authors, simply the ones whose track records in the used and rare book market have established them as collectible. In addition, a list of authors none of whose books are known to have a point of issue is included. Using this list and our companion guide, **A Pocket Guide to the Identification of First Editions**, the collector or dealer can identify first editions of those authors without difficulty.

Why this Guide.

Acquisition of books rarely takes place in the comfort of your reference library. Typically, the venue is a book sale, book fair, flea market, yard sale, auction, or in the home of someone offering books for sale. To equip the buyer with as much information as possible for these in-the-field situations, we first published **A Pocket Guide to the Identification of First Editions**. Using it, one can quickly determine whether a given book is a first edition or a later printing and differentiate book club editions from trade editions. But for the finer points, a second guide was needed.

Now, armed with both books, the collector or dealer can buy more intelligently and with more confidence.

This guide is not intended to supplant full-scale descriptive bibliographies of these authors. Indeed, it cannot. What this guide can do is help collectors, dealers, librarians, auctioneers, indeed anyone buying or selling collectible books, to identify more accurately the goods at hand. This guide reduces the risk of buying what one hopes is a first edition, first issue, only to find out later that it is not.

Points of Issue defined.

A *point of issue* occurs when a change is made in a book during the production of the first printing of the first edition without that change being noted as a change elsewhere in the book. Thus, some copies of the first printing exist without the change and some with it.

Production is the word choice because the process includes typesetting, printing, gathering, trimming, binding, stamping and the separate production of the dustjacket. Changes may occur at any stage of production, sometimes at several. These changes may be to correct an error of spelling, punctuation, typography or sequence; to alter something in the book, such as an illustration; to substitute one page for another; to add something inadvertently omitted or to alter the binding or its stamping. The result is a book that, on examination for the usual first edition identification method, appears to be a correct first edition. But because the change was made "invisibly," the collector must investigate further.

Williams, Tennessee. The Milk Train Doesn't Stop Here Anymore. Norfolk, 1964. 19-22: integral 22: *Scene Two*
Williams, Tennessee. One Arm and Other Stories. (Norfolk, 1949). CP: incorrect copyright credit by New Directions on integral leaf
Williams, Tennessee. The Rose Tattoo. (NY, 1951). B: rose cloth ST: black
Williams, Tennessee. Summer and Smoke. (Norfolk, 1948). DJ: back flap: 3 Williams plays listed
Williams, William Carlos. The Complete Collected Poems. 1906-1938. Norfolk, (1938). B: legal buckram dark green cloth
Williams, William Carlos. In the Money. Norfolk, Conn., (1940). *WHITE MULE* section not present
Williams, William Carlos. Kora in Hell: Improvisations. SF, (1957). 1st City Lights edition. BC: *printed in England at the Press of Villiers Publications, Holloway, London.*
Williams, William Carlos. Poems. (Rutherford, NJ), 1909. First poem.5: *of youth himself, all rose-y-clad* 9.3: *raptured*
Williams, William Carlos. Selected Poems (Norfolk, Conn., [1949]). EP: tan DJ: No mention of *The National Book Award*
Williams, William Carlos. White Mule. Norfolk, Conn., 1937. DJ: front flap: *June 10th*
Wilson, Colin. The Outsider. B, 1956. TP: date present
Wilson, Harry Leon. The Boss of Little Arcady. B, (1905). IM: *Lothrop Publishing Company*
Wilson, Harry Leon. The Seeker. NY, 1904. FC: gilt stamping
Wilson, Woodrow. Congressional Government. B, 1885. SP: publisher's monogram ADS: at end with 3 titles in *American Statesmen* list *In Preparation*
Wilson, Woodrow. The State: Elements of Historical and Practical Politics. B, 1889. FC: lettering slanted ADS: none at end
Wister, Owen. Roosevelt: The Story of a Friendship. NY, 1930. Prolog: *Karow* at head 100: *I went to my desk...*
Wodehouse, P.G. The Adventures of Sally. L, 1923. Verso of HT: nine titles ending with *The Girl on the Boat*

Whittier, John Greenleaf. Miriam and Other Poems. B, 1871. SP: *FO & Co.*

Whittier, John Greenleaf. The Panorama, and Other Poems. B, 1856. 52: page number present

Whittier, John Greenleaf. The Pennsylvania Pilgrim, and Other Poems. B, 1872. SP: monogram of *James R. Osgood & Co.*

Whittier, John Greenleaf. Poems. B, 1849. Il: last page of illustrations is blank 239: no note of an illustration of "*Star of Bethlehem*" and no such illustration in text

Whittier, John Greenleaf. Snow-Bound. A Winter Idyl. B, 1866. 52: page number at foot

Whittier, John Greenleaf. The Tent on the Beach and Other Poems. B, 1867. B: sides blindstamped with a single rule border SP: no blind-stamped rules at top or bottom IM: *Ticknor & Co.* 172:2 first letter *N* is perfect

Wieners, John. The Hotel Wently Poems. (SF), 1958. text censored Publisher's address: not *1334 Franklin Street*

Wiggin, Kate Douglas. Penelope's Irish Experiences. B & NY, 1901. B: (i-ii), (i) - (viii), (1) - 327, printer's imprint (328) (1/1, 2/4, 3-22/8, 23/4) 186.3up: *monthy*

Wilde, Oscar. The Picture of Dorian Gray. L, (1891). 208.8 up: *nd*

Wilde, Oscar. Poems. L, 1881. 136.stanza 2.3: *maid*

Wilde, Oscar. Ravenna. Newdigate Prize Poem. Oxford, 1878. B: grey wrappers FC & TP: *Oxford University* arms

Wilde, Oscar. Vera; Or, the Nihilists. L, 1880. B: grey wrappers

Wilder, Thornton. The Cabala. NY, 1926. 186.16: *doctors.* 196.13: *conversation* 202.12: *explaininn*

Williams, Tennessee. American Blues. (NY, 1948). FC: *Tennessee*

Williams, Tennessee. Androgyne, Mon Amour: Poems. NY, 1977. B: light green cloth EP: green

Williams, Tennessee. Cat on a Hot Tin Roof. (NY, 1955). Verso of title-leaf: no credit to The New York Times for a previous appearance of the foreword xii: no credit to Joseph Mielziner & Lucinda Ballard for scene & costume design

---

Since most collectors prefer the earliest possible state of the book, the book must be checked to see if a point of issue exists. In some cases, there are as many as four states of the first edition, each with differing value. This guide lists only the first issue points for most titles.

First Edition, First Issue, First State.

Our companion guide, **A Pocket Guide to the Identification of First Editions**, will assist you in determining whether a book is a first edition or a later printing. Naturally, any book must first meet the qualifications in that guide before **Points of Issue** comes into use.

First Issue is used synonymously with *First State* here, for the sake of economy. *First Issue* has been hairsplit to mean only points corrected after some copies have been circulated, while *First State* to mean a correction made before any distribution has occurred.

False Firsts.

Over the past fifty years or so, the Book Clubs have issued books nearly identical with the trade editions, but with a blind or colored deboss located in the lower corner of the back cover near the spine. The deboss, or indentation, has taken the form of a square, circle, dot, crown, etc. The problem is that a fair number of Book Club editions masquerade as true firsts, even saying so on the copyright pages. And when a False First is married to a trade edition dustjacket, it is even easier to be fooled. We have listed as many of these False Firsts as we know about, but there may be many more, so it is always wise to examine the back cover of the book to see if a Book Club deboss is present.

Dustjackets and Marriages.

Because dustjackets are not attached to their books, they move easily from a later printing to a first edition. This is called *marrying* (the book to the jacket). While a first edition is always more valuable with its dustjacket, these marriages must be done with discretion.

Frequently, a dustjacket will not change between printings, often because the publisher will print, say, 10,000 jackets, yet only publish 4000 copies in the first edition of the book. Leftover jackets are put on later printings. This makes economic sense since the jacket is a single sheet and the majority of the initial cost is prepress work; once the press is running, the unit cost is reduced substantially by a longer press run. Marrying a jacket from a later copy to a first is acceptable; some, but not all, dealers indicate this act by stating "jacket supplied."

However, many publishers print approximately equal numbers of jackets and books, and do the same for subsequent printings. Thus, many jackets are changed from the first to the second or later printings; a new printing of the jacket allows the publisher to use it for marketing by adding review quotes, literary prize nominations, film deals, altered

Wharton, Edith. The House of Mirth. NY, 1905.
   PA: laid with vertical chain lines 13/16" apart
   CP: *Scribner Press*
Wharton, Edith. The Marne. NY, 1918. 128: no printing code
Wharton, Edith. A Son at the Front. NY, 1923. 244.6: *lips*
Wharton, Edith. The Valley Of Decision. NY, 1902.
   Printer: *Merrymount Press*
Whistler, James A.M. The Gentle Art Of Making Enemies.
   L, 1890. 17: signature mark *B* below *b* in *him* 161: butterfly device below *ll* in *Mallarme* 162: tail on butterfly device points up and to the right
Whistler, James A.M. Mr. Whistler's "Ten O'clock." L, 1888.
   IM: *Chatto & Windus* on *5*, and *Spottiswoode & Co.* on *31*
Whistler, James A.M. Notes - Harmonies - Nocturnes.
   Chelsea, 1884. TP: *May, 1884*
White, Stewart Edward. Gold. GC, 1913. B: yellow cloth End of book: *Life of White* lacks illustrations, has decorative border around text
White, William Allen. The Autobiography Of... NY, 1946.
   CP: *H. Wolff*
Whitman, Walt. After All Not To Create Only. B, 1871.
   B: bevelled cloth boards, 8vo.
Whitman, Walt. An American Primer. B, 1904.
   B: vellum boards
Whitman, Walt. Drum Taps. NY, 1865.
   "When Lilacs Last in the Dooryard Bloom'd" not included
Whitman, Walt. Leaves Of Grass. NY, 1855.
   EP: marbled ST: gilt triple line border on FC and BC
Whitman, Walt. Memoranda During the War. Camden, New Jersey, 1875. IL: two portraits present
Whitman, Walt. Walt Whitman's Diary in Canada. B, 1904.
   B: grey boards, vellum back & corners
Whitman, Walt. The Wound Dresser. B, 1898.
   TP: publisher's device is slightly off-center CP: *1897*
Whittier, John Greenleaf. At Sundown ...With Designs by E.H. Garrett. B and NY, 1892. 46.11-12: lines approximately same length 52.1: *lark sings,* IL: final plate listed at *64*
Whittier, John Greenleaf. Legends of New England.
   Hartford, 1831. 98:last: *The go*

Wells, H.G. The Time Machine. L, 1895. ADS: at end, 16 pages in grey cloth issue w/blue spine stamping & purple front cover stamping; simultaneous blue wrapper issue: no ads
Wells, H.G. Tono-Bungay. L,1909. ADS: at end, 8 pp.,dated *1.09*.
Wells, H.G. Twelve Stories and a Dream. L, 1903.
ADS: at end, 22 pages, dated *20/9/03*.
Wells, H.G. The War of the Worlds. L, 1898.
ADS: at end, 16 pages, dated *1897*.
Wells, H.G. The Wheels of Chance. L, 1896. ADS: 10 pages, at end, dated *Oct. 1896*. 314: printer's imprint present
Wells, H.G. The Wonderful Visit. L, 1895.
B: red buckram, covers blank
Welty, Eudora. The Bride of the Innisfallen. NY, (1955).
CP: *copyright... 1955, by Eudora Welty.*
Welty, Eudora. The Golden Apples. L, (1950).
B: brown cloth   FEP: none
Welty, Eudora. Of Eudora Welty. NY, (1980). CP: *B C D E*
No usual Harcourt, Brace Jovanovich *first edition*
Welty, Eudora. The Wide Net. NY, (1943). TE: stained green
West, Nathanael. A Cool Million. The Dismantling of Lemeul Pitkin. NY, (1934). B: light tan cloth
West, Nathanael. Miss Lonelyhearts. NY, (1933). TP: Liveright publisher's device present CP: *at the Van Rees Press*
West, Paul. The Pearl and the Pumpkin. NY, (1904).
EP: pictorial, blue ink
Westcott, Edward Noyes. David Harum. NY, 1898.
40.next to last: *Julius* perfect
Wharton, Edith. The Age of Innocence. NY, 1920.
DJ: no Columbia (Pulitzer) Prize announcement
186: quote from the burial
Wharton, Edith. The Children. NY, 1928. CP: *First Printing, September, 1928* 347.(I): 122.23: *you... my* 135.14: *motors*
Wharton, Edith. Ethan Frome. NY, 1911.
TE: gilt   135.21: *wearily* perfect
Wharton, Edith. Fighting France: From Dunkerque To Belfort. NY, 1915. FC: *Fighting France* in gilt
Wharton, Edith. The Greater Inclination. NY, 1899.
257: *Merrymount Press* SP: *Wharton* only

---

biographical information, etc. While reviews alone do not guarantee a jacket is a later one, investigation should follow to determine if a jacket exists without reviews.

Values and this Guide.

Points of Issue is not a value guide. Second issues of some books are still valuable and collectible; second issues of others are worth a small fraction of the first issue. So if you have a second issue, it does not necessarily mean you have a worthless book, just a book, compared with the first issue, worth less.

How to Use this Guide.

Listings are alphabetical. Following the author, title, city and year, the points of issue are listed in the order in which the collector may encounter them, book first, then dustjacket: spine, binding, stamping, front cover, back cover, edges, endpapers, half-title, frontispiece, title page, copyright page, dedication page, text and line, advertisements and dustjacket.

Material in *italics* is understood to be the actual text to be sought when determining an issue point, though the text in the book being examined may or may not actually be in italics.

For the sake of economy, the locations of points are abbreviated in the **Key to the Listings** on the inside back cover for handy reference.

Authors without points.

All books to date by these authors are either first editions or later printings. None contain points of issue.

Adams, Leonie	Cain, James M.	Exley, Frederick
Ammons, A. R.	Cain, Paul	Faust, Irvin
Anderson, Maxwell	Caldwell, Erskine	Fearing, Kenneth
Arnow, Harriette Simpson	Carroll, Paul	Fitzgerald, Zelda
	Carruth, Hayden	Flanner, Janet
Attaway, William	Carson, Rachel	Foote, Shelby
Baker, Dorothy	Carter, Hodding	Fox, William Price
Basso, Hamilton	Charyn, Jerome	Friedman, Bruce Jay
Beagle, Peter S.	Ciardi, John	Fuchs, Daniel
Beattie, Ann	Clark, Tom	Gaines, Ernest J.
Beer, Thomas	Coates, Robert M.	Garrett, George
Berrigan, Daniel	Coker, Elizabeth Boatwright	Gass, William H.
Berrigan, Ted		Gellhorn, Martha
Berry, Wendell	Condon, Richard	Gill, Brendan
Bianchi, Martha	Connell, Evan S., Jr.	Gold, Herbert
Bishop, Elizabeth	Conroy, Jack	Gordimer, Nadine
Bishop, John Peale	Coover, Robert	Gores, Joe
Black, Mackinght	Corman, Sid	Goyen, William
Blechman, Burt	Crosby, Caresse	Grafton, Sue
Bogan, Louise	Crosby, Harry	Green, Hannah
Booth, Philip E.	Cullen, Countee	Greenberg, Joanne
Bourjaily, Vance	Dabbs, James McBride	Gregor, Arthur
Brace, Gerald Warner		Grimes, Martha
Breslin, Jimmy	DeLillo, Don	Grossman, Arthur
Brodeur, Paul	Dewey, John	Grubb, Davis
Bromfield, Louis	Dexter, Colin	Grumbach, Doris
Bronk, William	Dugan, Alan	Hammett, Dashiell
Brossard, Chandler	Dykeman, Wilma	Hale, Nancy
Brown, Alice	Eastlake, William	Hard, John Edward
Bryan, C. D. B.	Eberhart, Richard	Harris, Mark
Bryher, Winifred	Elkin, Stanley	Harrison, Jim
Buechner, Frederick	Elliott, George P.	Hazo, Samuel
Burke, James Lee	Ellison, Ralph	Hazzard, Shirley
Busch, Frederick	Ely, David	Hellman, Lillian

Wells, H.G. The Dream. L, (1924). TP: ad for Wells's titles preceding, with *All these are in print and on sale, whatever a lazy bookseller may say to the contrary at bottom* TE: plain

Wells, H.G. The First Men on the Moon. L, 1901.
   B: dark blue cloth, gilt stamping

Wells, H.G. The Food of the Gods. L, 1904.
   ADS: at end, 18 pages dated *20/7/04*

Wells, H.G. The Future in America. L, 1906.
   B: light reddish brown cloth, gilt stamping

Wells, H.G. Honors Physiography. L, 1893.
   ADS: 4 pages at end   B: brown cloth

Wells, H.G. In the Days of the Comet. L, 1906.
   ADS: at end, 8 pages, dated 5.5.06.

Wells, H.G. The Invisible Man. A Grotesque Romance.
   L, 1897. 1: numbered *2*   ADS: at end, 2 pages

Wells, H.G. The Island of Dr. Moreau. L, 1896. ADS: at end, ad for *The Time Machine* and 32 pages of other ads

Wells, H.G. Kipps. The Story of a Simple Soul. L, 1905.
   ADS: at end, 8 pages, dated *16/8/05*.

Wells, H.G. The New Machiavelli. L, 1911.
   Fore-edges and bottom edges untrimmed

Wells, H.G. The Peace of the World. L, n.d. B: grey wrappers

Wells, H.G. The Plattner Story and Others. L, 1897.
   ADS: at end, 40 pages dated *March 1897*.

Wells, H.G. The Research Magnificent. L, 1915.
   ADS: at end, dated *15.8.15*

Wells, H.G. The Sea Lady. A Tissue of Moonshine. L, 1902.
   ADS: at end, 40 pages, dated *July 1902*.

Wells, H.G. Select Conversations With an Uncle [now extinct] and Two Other Reminiscences. L, 1895.
   ADS: at end, 16 pages, dated *1895*.

Wells, H.G. The Stolen Bacillus and Other Incidents.
   L, 1895. ADS: at end, 32 pages, dated *Sept. 1895*.

Wells, H.G. Text-Book of Biology. L, n.d. 2 vols.
   Vol. I: ADS: 36 pages, at end, dated *19/9/92*.
   Vol. II: ADS: 32 pages, at end, dated *21/8/93*.
   B: dark green cloth

Warren, Robert Penn. All the King's Men. L, (1948).
   DJ: blue and white
Warren, Robert Penn. All the King's Men. NY, (1946).
   DJ: BC: *What Sinclair Lewis says...*
Warren, Robert Penn. Modern Rhetoric. NY, (1949).
   CP: *A present*
Warren, Robert Penn. A Plea in Mitigation.
   Macon, GA, 1966. 5.2: *abstation*
Warren, Robert Penn. Remember the Alamo. NY, (1958).
   B: blue-green cloth ADS: 2 pages at rear and on inside of DJ for 85 Landmark Books and 38 World Landmark Books DJ: 195/195
Waugh, Evelyn. Brideshead Revisited. B, 1946. B: blue cloth
   CP: *First edition after ... 600 copies - Published January 1946*
   DJ: back flap: no "*Printed in U.S.A.*"
Waugh, Evelyn. Decline and Fall. L, 1928. CP: *Originally publ...*
   September 1928 168-169: *Martin Gaythorn-Brodie and Kevin Saunderson respectively*
Waugh, Evelyn. Mr. Loveday's Little Outing and Other Sad Stories. L, (1936). B: red and black cloth ST: gilt
Waugh, Evelyn. Ninety-Two Days. L, 1934. SP: gilt lettering
Waugh, Evelyn. The Ordeal of Gilbert Pinfold. B, (1957).
   DJ: clipped with *$3.75* stamped to left of clip
Waugh, Evelyn. Remote People. L, (1931). SP: gilt lettering
Waugh, Evelyn. Rossetti His Life and Works. L, 1928. SP: gilt
Waugh, Evelyn. Scoop, a Novel About Journalism. L, (1938).
   88.last: *s* in *as*   DJ: FC: Daily Beast logo in black letters
Waugh, Evelyn. Waugh in Abyssinia. L, (1936).
   163-164: not cancelled DJ: front flap: not pasted over
Weinbaum, Stanley G. Dawn of Flame. (Jamaica, NY, 1936).
   Introduction by Palmer (not Keating)
Wells, H.G. Bealby. A Holiday. L, (1915). B: blue cloth
   ADS: 4 pages, at end, dated *Spring 1915* and a 32-page catalogue dated *25.11.14.*
Wells, H.G. Certain Personal Matters. Covent Garden, 1898.
   ADS: at end, 32 pages, dated *Spring Season 1897.*
Wells, H.G. The Discovery of the Future. L, 1902.
   FC: *Anticipation*

Herbst, Josephine
Heyen, William
Higgins, George V.
Himes, Chester
Hoffman, Daniel
Holmes, John Clellon
Humphrey, William
Inge, William
Irving, John
Jackson, Charles
Jackson, Shirley
James, P. D.
Jones, Madison Percy
Jong, Erica
Josephson, Matthew
Kahn, Roger
Kelley, William Melvin
Kelly, Edith Summers
Kennedy, X. J.
Kennedy, William
Killens, John Oliver
Kinnell, Galway
Koch, Kenneth
Kunitz, Stanley
Larner, Jeremy
Levin, Ira
Lodge, George Cabot
Loeb, Harold
Lowell, Robert
Lumpkin, Grace
MacDonald, John D.
March, William
Markfield, Wallace
Markson, David
Marshall, Paule
Matheson, Richard
Matthiessen, Peter
McAlmon, Robert
McCarthy, Mary
McCoy, Horace
McGuane, Thomas
Meredith, William
Merwin, W. S.
Millar, Kenneth
Molloy, Robert
Morrison, Toni
Moss, Howard
Motley, Willard
Nash, Ogden
Nemerov, Howard
Newman, Frances
Newhouse, Edward
Nims, John Frederick
O'Brien, Tim
Ozick, Cynthia
Paley, Grace
Parker, Robert B.
Percy, William Alexander
Peterkin, Julia
Petry, Anne
Plath, Sylvia
Pollini, Francis
Portis, Charles
Rawlings, Marjorie Kinnan
Rechy, John
Reed, Ishmael
Richter, Conrad
Riding, Laura
Robbins, Tom
Roberts, Elizabeth Madox
Roethke, Theodore
Roth, Henry
Rothenberg, Jerome
Rushdie, Salman
Sackville-West, Vita
Sandoz, Mari
Schulberg, Budd
Scott, Evelyn
Settle, Mary Lee
Shapiro, Karl
Sheed, Wilfrid
Singer, Isaac Bashevis
Smith, Betty
Smith, Thorne
Snodgrass, W. D.
Solzhenitsyn, Aleksandr
Sontag, Susan
Sorrentino, Gilbert
Spackman, W. M.
Spencer, Elizabeth
Stewart, Donald Ogden
Stuart, Jesse
Summers, Hollis
Swados, Harvey
Tate, James
Traven, B.
Traver, Robert
Van Dyke, Henry
Vidal, Gore
Wallant, Edw. Lewis
Whittemore, Edward
Wilbur, Richard
Williams, John A.
Willingham, Calder
Wilson, Edmund
Woiwode, Larry
Wolff, Maritta
Wright, Harold Bell
Wright, James
Young, Marguerite

Gramercy!

Without the stamina, wisdom and diligence of Amy Arledge, this book would not exist. Amy was the Chief Researcher and spent many hours rooting out the essential facts from countless bibliographies and other sources. Once we got to type, her assiduous eye for detail prevented many an embarrassment.

Dedicatory.

This book is for Deide, the epitome of wifely patience amidst my schemes, and for Emily and Ross, my most uncommon and treasured children.

This book is also dedicated to the memories of Charles William Coddington and Leon Vinson Driskell, two unusual and compelling individuals, each of whose counsel and friendship in times past, contributed, quite unknowingly, to the result you hold in your hands.

Van Vechten, Carl. Music After the Great War. NY, 1915.
    B: lavender cloth, paper labels
Van Vechten, Carl. Music and Bad Manners. NY, 1916.
    B: green boards
Vonnegut, Kurt. Happy Birthday, Wanda June. NY, 1971.
    DJ: front flap: price present at top
Vonnegut, Kurt. Player Piano. NY, 1952.
    CP: Scribner's seal & *A*
Walker, Alice. The Color Purple. NY, (1982).
    DJ: back flap: one address
Walker, Alice. To Hell With Dying. San Diego, (1988).
    DJ: *$13.95*
Wallace, Lew. The Prince of India. NY, 1893.
    Vol. I: no dedication   B: rosary stamped in red
Waller, Robert James. The Bridges of Madison County. NY, (1992) DJ: *$14.95* on front flap Rear Flap: no statement: *An Alternate Selection of the Book-of-the-Month-Club...*
Waller, Robert James. Slow Waltz in Cedar Bend. NY, (1993). EP: olive green BC: Warner Brothers' logo embossed DJ: shiny gold; front flap: no ISBN; back cover: *51695* on bar code
Warner, Charles Dudley. Backlog Studies. B, 1873.
    PA: laid (vii): List of Illustrations
Warner, Charles Dudley. Baddeck, and That Sort of Thing. B, 1874. ADS: none
Warner, Charles Dudley, *and* **Twain, Mark. The Gilded Age: a Tale of Today.** Hartford, 1873. ADS at end: *truex inde* TP: artist White included (vii): *Eschol* at *Chapter V* xvi: final illustration numbered *211* 246.5 up: *Hallelujah* (no comma) 280.18: *Dr. Jackson.* (period present) 351.last: *would kill me if she could, thought the Colonel; but he* 353.1-2: *let him keep it. She looked down into his face, with a pitia-/ble tenderness, and said in a weak voice,* 403: no illustration
Warner, Charles Dudley. In the Levant. B, 1877. 374: blank leaf follows (ii): no ad for *C.D. Warner's writings*
Warner, Charles Dudley. Saunterings. B, 1872.
    ADS: 2 pages PA: bulk 1"

Twain, Mark. The Tragedy of Pudd'nhead Wilson and the Comedy of Those Extraordinary Twins. Hartford, 1894. TP: integrally bound, not on a stub FP: facsimile signature 1 7/16" wide Sheets bulk 1 1/8"

Twain, Mark. A Tramp Abroad. Hartford, 1880. C: blind stamped border about square at inner corners FP: *Moses* (not *Titian's Moses*) FP: underlying lines vertical

Twain, Mark. A True Story of the Recent Carnival of Crime. B, 1877. FC: *JRO&CO* monogram

Twain, Mark. What is Man? NY, 1906. 131: *ends thinks about/it.*

Tyler, Anne. If Morning Ever Comes. L, 1965.
DJ: front flap: *than* in quote

Updike, John. Assorted Prose. (L, 1965). DJ: price is *25 shillings*

Updike, John. Bech is Back. NY, 1982. DJ: front flap: *FPT* ;
DJ: back flap: *10/82* ; back panel: *394-52806-9*

Updike, John. The Carpentered Hen. NY, (1958).
DJ: mentions *2 children*

Updike, John. A Child's Calendar. NY, (1965).
CP: No usual Alfred A. Knopf *first edition*

Updike, John. The Coup. NY, 1978. TE: yellow

Updike, John. Earthworm. (Princeton, 1979).
Postcard with earliest issue: *God Bless* stanza 3:1

Updike, John. The Magic Flute. NY, (1962).
CP: No usual Alfred A. Knopf *first edition*

Updike, John. Marry Me. NY, 1976. DJ: BC: *394-40856-X*

Updike, John. The Music School. NY, 1966.
46.poetry extract: *the state of both his universities, / "The king, observing with judicious eyes,*

Updike, John. The Poorhouse Fair. NY, 1959. DJ: back flap: one paragraph of copy only, on John Updike

Updike, John. The Ring. NY, (1964).
CP: No usual Alfred A. Knopf *first edition*

Updike, John. The Same Door. NY, 1959.
DJ: *Also by John Updike The Poorhouse Fair*

Uris, Leon. Exodus. NY, 1958. DJ: back panel: *LEON URIS* next to photo, no mention of Negev Desert

Van Dyne, Edith. *See* **Baum, L. Frank.**

Van Vechten, Carl. In the Garret. NY, 1920. B: black boards

Abbey, Edward. The Fool's Progress. NY, 1988. DJ: front flap: *mist-infested* Back flap: *Mickey*

Abercrombie, Lascelles. The Epic. L, 1914. B: black cloth

Abercrombie, Lascelles. The Poems of Lascelles Abercrombie. L, 1930.
B: blue cloth, TEG, fore and lower edges uncut

Abercrombie, Lascelles. Thomas Hardy. L, 1912.
B: dark blue cloth ADS: none

Adams, Alice. Listening to Billie. NY, 1978.
CP: No ususal *First Edition* statement

Adams, Andy. The Log of a Cowboy. B, 1903. TP: dated
List of illustrations: Map showing the trail

Ade, George. (assorted plays published by Samuel French). NY,1923-4. All have address *28-30 W. 38th St.* on earliest printings

Ade, George. Ade's Fables. GC, 1914. v., foot: *Abe's Fables*

Ade, George. Forty Modern Fables. NY, 1901. IM: *R.H. Russell*

Ade, George. The Girl Proposition. NY, 1902. IM: *R.H. Russell*

Ade, George. People You Know. NY, 1903.
IM: *R. H. Russell* CP: *First Impression, April, 1903*

Ade, George. The Slim Princess. Ind, (1907).
CP: *April* and *Braunworth*

Agee, James. A Death in the Family. NY, (1957).
TP: printed in blue 80.first word: *walking*

Aiken, Conrad. The Charnel Rose Senlin. B, 1918.
B: dark blue cloth

Aiken, Conrad. The Coming Forth by Day of Osiris Jones. NY, 1931. 37: *The music* as section title; page integral

Akers, Floyd. *See* **Baum, L. Frank.**

Albee, Edward. The American Dream/The Death of Bessie Smith/Fam and Yam. NY, 1962. Dramatists Play Service edition. B: bright orange stiff wrappers

Albee, Edward. Tiny Alice. NY, . CP: no usual Atheneum *first edition*; later printings stated

Albee, Edward. The Zoo Story/The Death of Bessie Smith/The Sandbox. NY, (1960). DJ: *$2.75*

Albee, Edward. The Zoo Story and The Sandbox. (NY, 1960). Dramatists Play Service edition. BC: First two titles *John Brown's Body* and *Auntie Mame*

Alcott, Louisa May. Little Women. B, 1868-69.
    Part One: ADS: p.11 has book priced at *$1.25*
    Part. Two: iv: no notice: *Little Women, Part One*

Aldrich, Thomas Bailey. The Story of a Bad Boy. B,1870.
    14.20: *scattered*   197.10: *abroad*

Aldridge, James. Signed With Their Honour. L,1942.
    SP: *Richard Aldridge*

Alger, Horatio, Jr. Abraham Lincoln, the Backwoods Boy. NY, 1883.
    ADS: this book no. 2 in *Boyhood and Manhood* series

Alger, Horatio, Jr. Adrift in the City. Ph, (1865).
    IM: *Porter & Coates*

Alger, Horatio, Jr. Falling in with Fortune. NY, 1900.
    ADS: no Alger titles listed

Alger, Horatio, Jr. Fame and Fortune. Ph, 1904.
    No frontispiece   TP: *By* damaged

Alger, Horatio, Jr. Finding a Fortune. Ph, 1904.
    SP: interlocking script monogram

Alger, Horatio, Jr. The Five Hundred Dollar Check. NY, (1891). TP: *United Staes Book Co.* Spine: *Porter & Coates*

Alger, Horatio, Jr. Frank and Fearless. Ph, 1897. TP: *1897*

Alger, Horatio, Jr. From Canal Boy to President. NY, 1881.
    266-8 transposed   267: errata slip

Algren, Nelson. The Man With the Golden Arm. GC, 1949.
    DJ: no National Book Award sticker

Algren, Nelson. The Neon Wilderness. GC, 1947.
    DJ: ads for other titles on back

Allen, Hervey. Anthony Adverse. NY, 1933. 352.6: *Zavier*
    397.22: *found* repeated 1086.18: *ship*

Allen, Hervey. Ballads of the Border, the Weakling and Other Pictures of the Mobilization. (El Paso), 1916. TP: no publisher's imprint CP: *Hervey*
    BC: *McMath Printing co., El Paso, Texas*

Allen, Hervey. Israfel: The Life and Times of Edgar Allen Poe. NY, 1926. 259: wine glass in portrait

Allen, Hervey. Toward the Flame. NY, (1926).
    CP: publisher's monogram

Allen, James Lane. Aftermath. NY, 1986.
    ADS: none for *Aftermath*

Twain, Mark. The Innocents Abroad. Hartford, 1869.
    xvii-xviii: no page reference numbers xvii: last entry *Valedictory* 129: no picture of Napoleon III
    643: *Chapter XLI* 654: *Personal History*

Twain, Mark. Is Shakespeare Dead? NY, 1909.
    No inserted leaves after (151) mentioning *Greenwood's Shakespeare Problem* TE: gilt

Twain, Mark. King Leopold's Soliloquy. B, 1905.
    WR: dark green printing

Twain, Mark. Life on the Mississippi. B, 1883. 441: illus. of Mark Twain in flames 443: *The St. Louis Hotel*

Twain, Mark. The Man That Corrupted Hadleyburg. NY, 1900. Across top of covers: 1 1/2" Plate opp. 2: *Page 2*

Twain, Mark. Mark Twain's (Burlesque) Autobiography. NY, (1871). CP: no ad for *Ball, Black & Co.*

Twain, Mark. Mark Twain's Sketches: New and Old. Hartford, 1875. 120: footnote from 119 repeated
    299: *From Hospital Days* skit Erratum slip bound in

Twain, Mark. Merry Tales. NY, 1892.
    EP: decorated No portrait frontispiece

Twain, Mark, et al. The Niagara Book. Buffalo, 1893.
    CP: notice in 3 lines (226): blank

Twain, Mark. Personal Recollections of Joan of Arc. NY, 1896. ADS: *Memoirs of Barras Volumes III-IV, just ready*

Twain, Mark. The Prince and the Pauper. B, 1882.
    SP: rosette 1/8" below fillet CP: *Franklin Press*

Twain, Mark. Pudd'nhead Wilson's Calendar for 1894. NY, 1893. 5: *count for* 15: *$4.00 a year*
    Inner back wrapper: *Do not fail to read...*

Twain, Mark. Punch, Brothers, Punch! NY, (1878).
    TP: *Mark Twain* in a roman type 91.4 up: *health off;......could* 101: 13 lines of text only

Twain, Mark. Roughing It. Hartford, 1872. xi.3: *My* perfect
    19.1: *My* perfect 242.20-21: *premises-said he/was occupying his* 592: ad present

Twain, Mark. The $30,000 Bequest. NY, 1906. CP: no ad

Twain, Mark. Tom Sawyer Abroad. NY, 1894.
    SP: distance between *WEBSTER* and *TWAIN* is 5 3/8"

Turow, Scott. Pleading Guilty. NY, (1993). DJ: silver and gilt type embossed; no UPC code on back panel; no "*Printed in U.S.A.*" on rear flap
B: paper meets cloth spine at 4 1/2" from cover edge

Twain, Mark. Adventures of Huckleberry Finn. NY, 1885.
List of illus.: "*Him and another Man*"...88 57.23: *with the was* 143: *l* missing in *Col.* (lettering is part of the illustration) 143.7: *b* in *body* broken 283-284: bound in 283: fly-line of man's trousers a definite curve

Twain, Mark. The Adventures of Tom Sawyer. Hartford, 1876. Across top of covers: 1" PA: calendared HT: blank verso Preface: blank verso

Twain, Mark. The Celebrated Jumping Frog of Calaveras County and Other Sketches. NY, 1867. ADS: precede TP 66.last: *life* unbroken 198.last: *this* unbroken

Twain, Mark. Christian Science. NY & L, 1907. CP: *Christian Science* not in list (iii): eight lines of type FP: dated *(1906)* 3.9: *farmhouse* 5.14: *W* in *Why* standard weight

Twain, Mark. The Complete Essays of... Charles Neider, ed. GC, 1963. TP: in green & black DJ: rear flap: lacks ISBN# B: grey & black

Twain, Mark. A Connecticut Yankee in King Arthur's Court. NY, 1889.
(59) *S*-like ornament between *THE* and *KING*

Twain, Mark. An Extract From Captain Stormfield's Visit to Heaven. NY, 1909. Across top of covers: 3/4"

Twain, Mark. Following the Equator. Hartford, 1897.
TP: *Hartford* only

Twain, Mark. The Gilded Age. Hartford, 1873. ADS at end: *truex inde* TP: artist *White* included (vii): *Eschol* at *Chapter V* xvi: final illustration numbered *211* 246.5 up: *Hallelujah* (no comma) 280.18: *Dr. Jackson.* (period present) 351.last: *would kill me if she could, thought the Colonel; but he* 353.1-2: *let him keep it. She looked down into his face, with a pitia-/ble tenderness, and said in a weak voice,* 403: no illustration

Twain, Mark. How To Tell a Story and Other Essays. NY, 1897. 187.16: *ciper*

Allen, James Lane. Flute and Violin. NY, 1891.
Across top of covers: 1 1/16"

Allen, James Lane. The Heroine in Bronze. NY, 1912. TE: gilt

Allen, James Lane. A Kentucky Cardinal. NY, 1895.
ADS: none for *Aftermath* or *A Kentucky Cardinal*

Allen, James Lane. The Reign of Law: A Tale of the Kentucky Hemp Fields. NY, 1900. vii: *facing* not present before numerals IL: in photogravure

Anderson, Sherwood. Hello Towns! NY, 1929. 35.30: *fiugers*

Anderson, Sherwood. Horses and Men. NY, 1923. TE: orange

Anderson, Sherwood. Many Marriages. NY, 1923. TE: orange

Anderson, Sherwood. Mid-American Chants. NY, 1923.
2-3 of 1st gathering: integral

Anderson, Sherwood. Poor White. NY, 1920. TE: stained blue

Anderson, Sherwood. A Story Teller's Story. NY, 1924.
TE: stained yellow

Anderson, Sherwood. The Triumph of the Egg. NY, 1921.
TE: stained yellow

Anderson, Sherwood. Winesburg, Ohio. NY, 1919.
TE: yellow *or* unstained EP: map in front TP: rule around not broken 86.5: *lay* 251.3: *the* has broken type

Angelou, Maya. I Know Why the Caged Bird Sings. NY, 1969. BC: no BOMC deboss at lower corner near spine B: Top edge of pages stained magenta; pages bulk 15/16"

Arlen, Michael. The London Venture. L, 1920. TP: *1920*

Ashbery, John. The Double Dream of Spring. NY, 1970.
SP: round Size: 8 5/16 x 6 1/8"

Ashbery, John. Selected Poems. L, (1967).
CP: (c) 1957, 1959, 1960, 1961, 1962, by John Ashbery.

Atherton, Gertrude. The Conqueror. NY, 1902. ST: white and gilt on FC and SP 546: numeral in upper left

Atherton, Gertrude. The Gorgeous Isle. NY, 1908. EP: pictorial

Atherton, Gertrude. Ruler of Kings. NY, 1904.
B: brown cloth, gilt stamping FC: ornament

Atherton, Gertrude. A Whirl Asunder. NY, (1895). Height: 6"

Auchincloss, Louis. The Great World and Timothy Colt. B, 1956. DJ: front flap: *$3.75*

Auden, W.H. About the House. L, (1966).
    8: erratum slip tipped-in
Auel, Jean. The Clan of the Cave Bear. NY, (1980).
    DJ: front flap: *$12.95 ($15.95 is later)*
Bacheller, Irving. Eben Holden. B, (1900).
    SP: pine cone tops rounded, not flat
    400.13: *go to fur*
Bacheller, Irving. From Stories of Memory. NY, (1938).
    CP: publisher's monogram
Bacheller, Irving. Keeping Up With William. Ind, (1918).
    TP: "*I*" missing from *Indianapolis*
Bacheller, Irving. A Man for the Ages. Ind, 1919.
    CP: *Braunworth & Company*
Bahr, Jerome. All Good Americans. NY, 1937. B: blue cloth
    (1939 editions with *A* on CP are not first editions)
Baker, Elliott. A Fine Madness. NY, (1964).10:5up: *Fitzgerald*
Baker, George P. The Pilgrim Spirit. B, 1921. 74: *Brewster*
Baldwin, James. The Fire Next Time. NY, 1963.
    EP: black   B: off-white cloth   DJ: back flap: *The Dial Press, Inc. 461 Park Avenue South, New York 16*
    Bulk: 1 3/16" cover top to cover top, outer edges
Baldwin, James. Notes of a Native Son. B, (1965).
    DJ: no review quotes on back
Bangs, John Kendrick. The Booming of Acre Hill and Other Reminiscences of Urban and Suburban Life. NY & L, 1900. (267): *By Mark Twain Personal Recollections of Joan of Arc*
Bangs, John Kendrick. Coffee and Repartee. NY, 1893.
    (126): *Seven Dreamers*
Bangs, John Kendrick. The Idiot at Home. NY & L, 1900.
    (v): Chapters 2 & 3 listed at pages *13* and *27* respectively
Bangs, John Kendrick. Katharine a Travesty. (NY), 1888.
    47: *givest* (128): imprint in red
Bangs, John Kendrick. Mr. Bonaparte of Corsica. NY, 1895. (268): *By Brander Matthews. Vignettes of Manhattan...*
Bangs, John Kendrick. Mr. Munchausen. B, 1901.
    CP: *Small Maynard*   2nd CP: *Noyes, Platt* rubber-stamped   3rd CP: *Noyes, Platt* printed over *Small Maynard*   4th CP: *Noyes, Platt* only

Thompson, Ruth Plumly. Kabumpo in Oz. C, (1922).
    HT: pictorial of Kabumpo follows ownership leaf
    299: portrait of Princess Dorothy
    IL: color plates coated on printed side only
Thompson, Ruth Plumly. The Lost King of Oz. T, (1925).
    PA: heavy stock   IL: plates coated on printed side only
    193:4 top serif of *k* is unbroken
Thompson, Ruth Plumly. The Royal Book of Oz. C, (1921).
    IL: facing 255, misspelt caption *Scarecorw's*; plates coated on printed side only
Thurber, James. The Beast in Me and Other Animals. NY, (1948). 55.9 up: *burn*   63.2 up: *Pre.sident* not present
Thurber, James. Lanterns and Lances. NY, (1961).
    BC: no book club deboss at lower corner near spine
Thurber, James. Let Your Mind Alone. NY and L, 1937.
    B: drawing on FC: line around dots in motorman's cheek and extra line curving down from top of head to ear
Thurber, James. The Thurber Carnival. NY, (1948).
    vi: *xi* not aligned   25.7: *prettily*   171: *H* curved
Tidyman, Ernest. Dummy. B, (1974).
    BC: no book club deboss at lower corner near spine
Tolkien, J.R.R. The Hobbit, Or There and Back Again. L, 1937. DJ: rear flap: *Dodgeson* with publisher's handwritten correction
Tolkein, J.R.R. A Middle English Vocabulary. Oxford, 1922.
    ADS: *October 1922*   TP: *Printed in England* not present
Tolkien, J.R.R. The Silmarillion. B, 1977.
    List of "Books By:" *Father Giles of Ham*
Tomlinson, H.M. All Our Yesterdays. L, 1930.
    67: *Our All Yesterdays*   237: omission of part of text
    359: omission of part of text
Tomlinson, H.M. The Sea and the Jungle. L, (1912).
    ADS: 10 leaves at back
Toole, John Kennedy. A Confederacy of Dunces. Baton Rouge, 1980. DJ: back panel: no review comment in strip above brick wall
Tryon, Thomas. The Other. NY, 1971.
    DJ: edge of back flap: *394-46792-2*

Theroux, Paul. The Family Arsenal. B, 1976.
    DJ: front flap: *0876*
    BC: no book club deboss at lower corner near spine
Theroux, Paul. The Great Railway Bazaar / By Train Through Asia. B, 1975. CP: number sequence with *1*
Theroux, Paul. Picture Palace. B, 1978.
    DJ: silver stamping, black background
    BC: no book club deboss at lower corner near spine
Thomas, Dylan. The Collected Poems of Dylan Thomas. (NY, 1953). 199: *daugher*
Thomas, Dylan. The Doctor and the Devils and Other Scripts. (NY, 1966). DJ: BC: ad for *Collected Poems*
Thomas, Dylan. 18 Poems. L, (1934). SP: flat
Thomas, Dylan. The Map of Love. L, (1939).
    B: fine grained mauve cloth, silky texture
Thomas, Dylan. Quite Early One Morning. L, 1954.
    3 & 11:end of verse 5: full stop after *sailors*
Thomas, Dylan. Selected Writings. (NY, 1946). B: green cloth
    TP: double page spread CP: *Copyright 1946...*
    DJ: back panel: "*The New Classics Series...*" & "*333 Sixth Avenue*" absent
Thomas, Ross. The Fools in Town Are On Our Side. NY, 1971. DJ: back cover: review of *The Singapore Wink*
Thomas, Ross. Protocol For a Kidnapping. NY, 1971.
    B: red and tan boards
Thompson, A.C. Preludes. L, 1875. EP: brown
Thompson, Francis. Poems. L. 1893. ADS: *October*
Thompson, Hunter S. Fear and Loathing: On the Campaign Trail. (SF, 1973). DJ: *$6.95*; white border around picture on back panel
Thompson, Maurice. Alice of Old Vincennes. Ind, (1900).
    1: folio present   Running heads: bold-face capitals
    Last p: no *Acknowledgments*
Thompson, Ruth Plumly. The Cowardly Lion of Oz. C, (1923).
    IL: plates coated on printed side only
Thompson, Ruth Plumly. The Giant Horse of Oz. C, (1928).
    Frontispiece: *Oniberon*
    IL: color plates coated on printed side only

Bangs, John Kendrick. Over the Plum Pudding. NY & L, 1901. FP: oval form
Bangs, John Kendrick. A Rebellious Heroine a Story. NY, 1896. 49: signature mark *4* present
Baring, Maurice. Landmarks in Russian Literature. L, n.d.
    ADS: at end, dated *February, 1910*
Baring, Maurice. Russian Essays and Stories. L, n.d.
    ADS: at end, dated *August, 1908*
Baring, Maurice. With the Russians in Manchuria. L, n.d.
    ADS: at end, dated *March, 1905*
Baring, Maurice. A Year in Russia. L, n.d.
    ADS: at end, dated *October, 1906*
Barnes, Djuna. Ladies Almanack. NY, (1972).
    1st reissue. [90]: 72 73 74 10987654321
Barnes, Julian. Duffy. L, (1980). DJ: *4.95 pounds*
Barnes, Julian. Flaubert's Parrot. L, (1984). DJ: colors on upper panel are incorrectly printed
Barrie, James M. Auld Licht Idylls. L, 1888.
    ADS: 2 pages at end
Barrie, James M. An Edinburgh Eleven. L, 1889.
    B: wrappers   FC: *Gavin Ogilvy* TP: *J. M. Barrie*
Barrie, James M. Half Hours. L, n.d. 1: *The Kirrlemuir Edition of / the Works of J. M. Barrie*
Barrie, James M. The Little Minister. L, 1891.
    (3 vols.) Last P. text each volume: no numbers beneath imprint   End of volume I: 16 pages of ads
Barrie, James M. Mary Rose. L, 1924. TP: *1924*
Barrie, James M. Peter and Wendy. NY, 1911.
    PA: English sheets
Barrie, James M. Quality Street. L, (1901).
    CP: *Copyright in its dramatic form, 1901.*
Barrie, James M. Sentimental Tommy. L, 1896.
    ADS: dated *6G-8.96*
Barrie, James M. A Tillyloss Scandal. NY, (1893).
    Publisher's address: *43, 45, 47, East 10th Street*
Barrie, James M. When a Man's Single. L, 1888.
    ADS: 2 pages at end
Barth, John. Giles Goat-boy. GC, 1966.   Foot, last P.: H18   No copy observed with usual Doubleday *First Edition* on CP

Barrie, James M. When a Man's Single. L,1888.
    ADS: 2 pages at end
Barth, John. Giles Goat-boy. GC, 1966. Foot, last P.: H18 No copy observed with usual Doubleday *First Edition* on CP
Barthelme, Donald. City Life. NY, (1970).
    BC: no book club deboss at lower corner near spine
    DJ: glossy paper Back Panel: *0462* not present
Baum, L. Frank. The Daring Twins. C, (1911).
    FC: design by Hazenplug shows twins full-length
Baum, L. Frank. Dorothy and the Wizard in Oz. C, (1908).
    SP: *The Reilly & Britton Co.*
Baum, L. Frank. The Enchanted Island of Yew. Ind, (1903).
    CP: *Braunworth* imprint 238: illustration incorrectly positioned
Baum, L. Frank. John Dough and the Cherub. C, (1906).
    275:10 *cage* SP: *The Reilly & Britton Co.* Detachable contest blank for *"The Great John Dough Mystery"* on yellow paper facing p. 8
Baum, L. Frank. The Last Egyptian. Ph, 1908.
    CP: no imprint; *Published May 1, 1908*
Baum, L. Frank. The Life and Adventures of Santa Claus. Ind, (1902). Section Headings: *Book First, Book Second* and *Book Third* IL: dedication leaf and first page of Table of Contents are the only textual illustrations
Baum, L. Frank. Little Bun Rabbit and Other Stories. C, (1916). ADS: no ads for series on back of ownership leaf
Baum, L. Frank. The Lost Princess of Oz. C, (1917).
    ADS: list ends with *The Lost Princess of Oz*
Baum, L. Frank. The Magic of Oz. C, (1919).
    ADS: list ends with *The Tin Woodman of Oz*
Baum, L. Frank. The Magical Monarch of Mo. Ind, (1903).
    EP: no orange & black pictorials IL:(21) undamaged
    CP: IM in upper & lower case serif type
    50: numeral perfect
Baum, L. Frank. The Marvelous Land of Oz. C, 1904. CP: no *Published July, 1904* 4: dedication measures 6 1/4" IL: Two sets of text illustrations (22) & (27); (82) & (158)
    FC: title is in blue ink only

Tarkington, Booth. Beasley's Christmas Party. NY, 1909.
    SP: holly leaf present
Tarkington, Booth. Beauty and the Jacobin. NY,1912. CP: *I-M*
Tarkington, Booth. Cherry. NY & L, 1903.
    TP: date *1903* in design under *NEW YORK*
Tarkington, Booth. The Country Cousin. NY, (1921). 3.1: *in*
Tarkington, Booth. Gentle Julia. GC, 1922. FC: no silhouette
Tarkington, Booth. The Gentleman From Indiana. NY, 1899.
    245.12: last word *eye* 245.16: *so pretty heart*
    291.7: *brainy bumps* 342.23: *brain of Zeus*
Tarkington, Booth. The Magnificent Ambersons. GC, 1918.
    PA: all white Across sheets: 1 1/8" B: light brown
Tarkington, Booth. The Midlander. NY, 1924. CP: No usual Doubleday, Page *first edition* (publisher considered a preceding limited edition to be the first.)
Tarkington, Booth. Monsieur Beaucaire. NY, 1900.
    IM: *Gilliss Press* seal measures 1/2" diameter
Tarkington, Booth. Penrod. GC, 1914.
    B: light blue mesh cloth Across pages at top: 1 5/16"
    viii: so numbered 19.23: *sence*
Tarkington, Booth. Penrod and Sam. GC, 1916.
    Perfect type on 86, 141, 149, 210
Tarkington, Booth. The Plutocrat. Presentation Edition. GC, 1927. 26.running head: *Platocrat*
Tarkington, Booth. Seventeen. NY, (1916). CP: *B-Q*
Tarkington, Booth. The Turmoil. NY, 1915. CP: *A-P*
Tarkington, Booth. The Two Van Revels. NY, 1902.
    p.1 of ADS: *Monsieur Beaucaire 80th Thousand*
    p.3 of ADS: *70th Thousand* CP: *Published, October, 1902, R*
Tarkington, Booth. The Wren. NY, 1922.
    CP: *28-30 West 38th Street*
Tate, Allen. Jefferson Davis: His Rise and Fall. NY, 1929.
    B: black cloth FC & SP: printed labels EP: map
Taylor, Peter. In the Miro District. L, 1977. DJ: price in pounds
Tennyson, Alfred Lord. Poems, Chiefly Lyrical. L,1830. 91: *19*
Theroux, Alexander. Three Wogs. B, 1972. DJ: sepia-toned photo and back flap text reads *Trappist monaster in Kentucky*

Styron, William. In the Clap Shack. NY, (1973).
   CP: No usual Random House *First Edition*
Styron, William. The Long March. NY, (1952). FC: *A Modern Library Paperback*; no mention of *Set This House on Fire*; BC: Ad for *Modern Library Paperbacks*, P1 through P24 SP: *P22*   (Vintage Book paperbound edition is later.)
Styron, William. The Long March. NY, (1968). 1st hardbound ed. CP: no Random House *First Edition* DJ: front flap: *$3.95 and 3/68*; back flap: "*Confessions...*" mentioned
Summers, Montague. A Gothic Bibliography. L, (1940).
   IL: 22 plates
Summers, Montague. The Playhouse of Pepys. L, 1935. B: scarlet cloth SP: thick rule above three thin rules at foot
Swinburne, Algernon Charles. Astrophel and Other Poems. L, 1894. ADS: *February*
Swinburne, Algernon Charles. Atalanta in Calydon. L, 1865. Pages total 111 only
Swinburne, Algernon Charles. Chastelard: a Tragedy. L, 1865. IM: *Moxon*   ADS: *November*
Swinburne, Algernon Charles. Marino Faliero, a Tragedy. L, 1885. ADS: 32 pages
Swinburne, Algernon Charles. Poems and Ballads. L, 1866. IM: *E. Moxon*
Swinburne, Algernon Charles. The Queen-Mother and Rosamond. Two Plays. L, 1860. SP: *A.G. Swinburne*
Swinburne, Algernon Charles. Under the Microscope. L, 1872.   Suppressed leaf laid in
Swinburne, Algernon Charles. William Blake: a Critical Essay. L, 1868. TP: *Zamiel*
Symonds, John Addington. Giovanni Boccaccio as Man and Author. L, 1895. TE: plain though an ad at end says *gilt*
Symonds, John Addington. In the Key of Blue and Other Prose Essays. L, 1893. B: light blue cloth
Symonds, John Addington. An Introduction to the Study of Dante. L, 1872. B: red cloth Errata slip before p.1, text
Synge, John M. The Well of the Saints. L, 1905. No Yeats intro
Tarkington, Booth. Alice Adams. GC, 1921.
   419.14: *I can't see you why don't wear*

Baum, L. Frank. The Master Key. Ind, (1901). B: 8-page signatures CP: *The Bowen-Merrill Company* is 1 21/32" long
Baum, L. Frank. Mother Goose in Prose. C, (1897). B: 16-page signatures except for last two which are 8 pages and 4 pages respectively. Terminal leaf concludes on p. (268)
Baum, L. Frank. Ozma of Oz. C, (1907).
   IL: (221) printed in color SP: *The Reilly &/ Britton Co.*
Baum, L. Frank. The Patchwork Girl of Oz. C, 1913. B: light
Baum, L. Frank. Phoebe Daring. C, (1912).   B: shows heroine writing DJ: flap lists only 7 titles in "*Aunt Jane's*" series
Baum, L. Frank. Queen Zixi of Ix. NY, 1905.
   IL: 169-236 color-scheme of terra cotta and black
Baum, L. Frank. Rinkitink in Oz. C, (1916). ADS: none
Baum, L. Frank. The Road to Oz. C, (1909). PA: multi-colored 129: page number & caption present IM: *Reilly&Britton*
Baum, L. Frank. The Scarecrow of Oz. C, (1915).
   ADS: lists ends with *The Scarecrow of Oz*.
Baum, L. Frank. Sea Fairies. C, 1911. FC label: three heads
Baum, L. Frank. Tik-Tok of Oz. C, (1914). ADS: verso of half-title list ends with *The Patchwork Girl of Oz*
Baum, L. Frank. The Tin Woodman of Oz. C, (1918).
   ADS: list ends with *The Tin Woodman of Oz*
Baum, L. Frank. Woggle-bug Book. C, 1905.
   FC: blue stippled background BC: blank
Baum, L. Frank. The Wonderful Wizard of Oz. C & NY, 1900. SP: plain green imprint Verso of title-leaf: blank 14:1 *low wail on ...* Col: 11 lines IL: color plate facing p. 34 has 2 dark blots on moon; Scarecrow and Stork color plate facing p.92 has red horizon background
Baum, L. Frank, *writing as* **Floyd Akers. The Boy Fortune Hunters in Alaska.** C, (1908). ADS: on verso of TP: 3 titles 271: text ends *unvarying good fortune and The End*.
Baum, L. Frank, *writing as* **Floyd Akers. The Boy Fortune Hunters in Egypt.** C, (1908). TP: open book device above imprint ADS: on back of TP lists 3 titles in series; separate leaf at end lists *The Girl Graduate* 291: text ends *very rich indeed and The End*.

Baum, L. Frank, *writing as* **Floyd Akers. The Boy Fortune Hunters In Panama.** C, (1908). TP: open book device above imprint   AD: back of TP lists 3 titles in series   310: text ends with *powerless to control.*

Baum, L. Frank, *writing as* **Floyd Akers. The Boy Fortune Hunters In the South Seas.** C, (1911). AD: lists *The Daring Twins, Annabel* & 6 "*Aunt Jane's Nieces*" titles

Baum, L. Frank, *writing as* **Edith Van Dyne. Annabel.** C, (1906). B: 16-page signatures except for first one of 8 pages   SP: *The Reilly & / Britton Co.*

Baum, L. Frank, *writing as* **Edith Van Dyne. Aunt Jane's Nieces Abroad.** C, (1906). TE: stained green   EP: white

Baum, L. Frank, *writing as* **Edith Van Dyne. Aunt Jane's Nieces and Uncle John.** C, (1911). ADS: verso of half-title lists 6 titles in series & *Daring Twins* & *Annabel*

Baum, L. Frank, *writing as* **Edith Van Dyne. Aunt Jane's Nieces at Work.** C, (1909). TP: 3 previous titles listed

Baum, L. Frank, *writing as* **Edith Van Dyne. Aunt Jane's Nieces In Society.** C, (1910).
AD: back of half-title lists 5 titles in series

Baum, L. Frank, *writing as* **Edith Van Dyne. Aunt Jane's Nieces In the Red Cross.** C, (1915).
CP: single notice

Baum, L. Frank, *writing as* **Edith Van Dyne. Aunt Jane's Nieces on the Beach.** C, (1913).
AD: verso of half-title lists 8 titles

Baum, L. Frank, *writing as* **Edith Van Dyne. Aunt Jane's Nieces on Vacation.** C, (1912).
AD: verso of half-title, lists 7 titles

Baum, L. Frank, *writing as* **Edith Van Dyne. Aunt Jane's Nieces Out West.** C, (1914).
AD: verso of half-title lists 9 titles

Baum, L. Frank, *writing as* **Edith Van Dyne. Daughters of Destiny.** C, (1906). B: pictorial cover label above gilt-stamped title and author's name

Baum, L. Frank, *writing as* **Edith Van Dyne. The Fate of a Crown.** C, (1905). 306: final leaf of text   Each chapter begins on a recto, the previous verso often blank   IL: plates not included in pagination

Stevenson, Robert Louis. Treasure Island. L, 1883.
ADS: *July, 1883*

Stevenson, Robert Louis. Underwoods. L, 1887. ADS: *July*

Stevenson, Robert Louis. Virginibus Puerisque and Other Papers. L, 1881. ADS: *8.80*

Stockton, Frank. The Bee-Man of Orn, etc. NY, 1887. PA: laid

Stockton, Frank. Buccaneers and Pirates of Our Coasts. NY and L, 1898. TP: integral   CP: notice is 2 lines in name of the Macmillan Company

Stockton, Frank. The Casting Away of Mrs. Lecks and Mrs. Aleshine. NY, (1886).
Signature #s at 9,25,49,57,73,81,97,105,121,125

Stockton, Frank. The Clocks of Rondaine and Other Stories. NY, 1892. (ii): six titles listed

Stockton, Frank. The Great War Syndicate. NY, 1889. WR: *Collier's Once a Week... In this No. 21 Frank R. Stockton commences his new...*   IM: *Collier*

Stockton, Frank. The Late Mrs. Null. NY, 1886. 150.23: *mattrass*

Stockton, Frank. Pomona's Travels. NY, (1894). SP: publisher's monogram   ST: gilt & black   B: green cloth

Stockton, Frank. Rudder Grange. NY, 1879. ADS: *Mrs. Frances Hodgson Burnett's Earlier Stories* (1): signature mark *I* present   No ads for or reviews of this title   18 chapters

Stockton, Frank. The Rudder Grangers Abroad and Other Stories. NY, 1891.
ADS: precede TP and contain no mention of this title

Stockton, Frank. Stockton's Stories: Second Series. The Christmas Wreck and Other Stories. NY, 1886.
TP: & B: *Stockton's stories: Second Series* present

Stoker, Bram. Dracula. Westminster, 1897. ADS: none present

Strachey, Lytton. Landmarks of French Literature. L, (1912). TE: green

Stribling, T.S. Birthright. NY, 1922. 168.11-12: *transposed*

Stribling, T.S. East Is East. NY, (1928).
B: cloth, not pictorial boards

Stribling, T.S. Fombombo. NY, 1923. CP: *The Ridgway Co.*

Sturgeon, Theodore. Without Sorcery. NY, 1948.
29-page brochure titled *it* present

Steinbeck, John. The Wayward Bus. NY, 1947.
B: deep reddish brown cloth
BC: no book club deboss at lower corner near spine
CP: *Printed in the U.S.A. by The Haddon Craftsman*

Stephen, Leslie. Samuel Johnson. L, 1878.
ADS: *English Men of Letters* series only 13: *Letty*

Stephens, James. Arthur Griffith. Journalist and Statesman. Dublin, n.d. WR: tan

Stephens, James. The Demi-Gods. L, 1914. HT: present

Stephens, James. Five New Poems. L, 1913.
WR: magenta with uncolored designs

Sterling, George. Beyond the Breakers and Other Poems.
SF, 1914. 24.7: *stands*

Sterling, George. The Caged Eagle. SF, 1916.
34: *To* 162: *scourse*

Sterling, George. The House of Orchids and Other Poems.
SF, 1911. 31.9: *Langourous* 48.12: *omniponent*

Sterling, George. A Wine of Wizardry and Other Poems.
SF, 1909. FC: gilt decoration

Stevens, Wallace. Harmonium. NY, 1923. B: red, yellow, blue & white checkered paper-covered boards

Stevens, Wallace. Ideas of Order. NY,1936. B: pink,yellow, grey & white vertically striped paper-covered boards SP: cloth

Stevens, Wallace. The Man with the Blue Guitar. NY, 1937.
DJ: front flap: *conjunctioning*

Stevenson, Robert Louis. Island Nights' Entertainment.
L, 1893. List of author's works: p.ii: price list changed in ink by hand from five to six shillings

Stevenson, Robert Louis. Kidnapped. L, 1886. B: blue cloth
40.11: *business* 312: Ad for *The Illustrated Treasure Island*, and 16 unnumbered pages of ads

Stevenson, Robert Louis. New Arabian Nights. L, 1882. 2 vols.
Vol. I: EP: yellow Vol. II: 155: *55* 179: *Maledroit*
ADS: 32 pages at end, dated *May 1882*

Stevenson, Robert Louis. The Silverado Squatters. L, 1883.
Back: 32-page catalog dated *1883*

Stevenson, Robert Louis. The Strange Case of Dr. Jekyll and Mr. Hyde. L, 1886. B: wrappers
FC: date altered in ink by hand from *1885* to *1886*

Baum, L. Frank, *writing as* **Edith Van Dyne. The Flying Girl.**
C, (1911). FC: ST: white SP: lettering stamped white

Baum, L. Frank, *writing as* **Edith Van Dyne. The Flying Girl and Her Chum.** C, (1912).
FC: ST: title is white SP: white lettering

Baum, L. Frank, *writing as* **Edith Van Dyne. Mary Louise.** C, (1916). FC: title stamped in dark blue outline & white

Baum, L. Frank, *writing as* **Edith Van Dyne. Mary Louise in the Country.** C, (1916).
FC: *Mary Louise* stamped in dark blue outline and white

Baum, L. Frank, *writing as* **Edith Van Dyne. Sam Steele's Adventures on Land and Sea.** C, (1906). PA: laid

Beach, Rex. The Spoilers. NY, 1906. SP: *Rex E. Beach*

Beckett, Samuel. How It Is. NY, (1964).
DJ: rear flap: no roman numeral *ii* or larger

Beebe, William. Jungle Peace. NY, 1918.
No Teddy Roosevelt intro

Beebe, William. Log of the Sun. NY, 1906. Edges: gilt

Beebe, William. Two Bird-Lovers in Mexico. B, 1905.
FC: *Charles M. Beebe* 2nd issue FC: *C. William Beebe*
3rd issue FC: gold sky background absent
4th issue FC: no pictorial design, lettering only

Beerbohm, Max. The Happy Hypocrite: a Fairy Tale. NY & L, 1897. FC: period present Col: dated *December 1896*

Beerbohm, Max. The Poet's Corner. L,1904.
B: pictorial boards

Beerbohm, Max. Seven Men. L, 1919. B: bright blue cloth

Beerbohm, Max. Zuleika Dobson. L, 1911.
B: rough brown cloth preferred

Bell, Clive. Enjoying Pictures. L, 1934. Plate IV: C.R.W. Nevinson's "War Scene" and footnote present

Bellamy, Edward. Looking Backward. 2000-1887. B, 1888. B: green cloth CP: printer's imprint 210.8: *wore*

Bellow, Saul. The Adventures of Augie March. NY, 1953.
TE: orange CP: *Vail-Ballou* DJ: no review quotes BC: no deboss at lower right corner FF: DJ must have ad on rear inner flap

Bellow, Saul. Henderson the Rain King. NY, 1959. DJ: back panel: white square headed *Saul Bellow as a novelist*

Bellow, Saul. Herzog. NY, (1964). B: poorly printed grey initial letters at start of each chapter   DJ: back panel: no reviews

Bellow, Saul. Humboldt's Gift. NY, (1975). DJ: front flap: *0875*   DJ: back flap: *Publishers of The Viking Portable Library and Viking Compass paperbacks*   BC: no crown deboss at bottom   B: yellow paper over boards w/gold cloth

Benet, Stephen Vincent. Five Men and Pompey. B, 1915. WR: purple

Bennett, Arnold. A Man From the North. L, 1898. ADS: announces this title; dated *1897*

Berger, Thomas. Crazy in Berlin. NY, (1958). No rear flyleaf

Berryman, John. The Dispossessed. NY, (1948). CP: *First printing*

Betjeman, John. Ghastly Good Taste. L, 1933. 119-20: cancel

Bierce, Ambrose. Black Beetles in Amber. SF & NY, 1892. IM: *Western Authors Publishing Company*

Bierce, Ambrose. The Cynic's Word Book. NY, 1906. No frontispiece

Bierce, Ambrose. Fantastic Fables. NY, 1899. B: light brown cloth, pictorial stamping

Bierce, Ambrose. Shapes of Clay. SF, 1903. 71.5-6: *We've nothing better here than bliss. Walk in.But I must tell you this:*

Bierce, Ambrose. Write In Right. NY,1909. Page size: 5 3/4"x3"

Bierce, Ambrose, *writing as* **Dod Grile. The Fiend's Delight.** NY, 1873. ADS: none in back

Bierce, Ambrose, *writing as* **William Herman. The Dance of Death.** (SF, 1877). No press notices at back

Blatty, William Peter. The Exorcist. NY, 1971. DJ: front flap: no reviews   DJ: back panel: photo of author w/coffee cup

Blunden, Edmund. The Waggoner. L, 1920. B: blue cloth

Bodenheim, Maxwell. Minna and Myself. NY, 1918. 67.35: *Posner*

Bowen, Elizabeth. Collected Impressions. L, (1950). ix: misnumbered *x*

Bowen, Elizabeth. The House in Paris. NY, 1936. CP: *First American Edition* (not *published May 1936*)

Bowles, Paul. A Little Stone. L, (1950). B: light green

Boyd, James. Drums. NY & L, 1925. TP: both cities stated

Boyd, James. Marching On. NY,1927. CP: no printing statement

Stein, Gertrude. Geography and Plays. B, (1922). B: title & author's name on cover, light grey paper over boards   ST: dark blue on cover

Stein, Gertrude. Lectures in America. NY, (1935). B: beige glazed cloth   TE: dark grey   FP: present   PA: beveled edges

Stein, Gertrude. Paris France. NY, 1940. B: deep rose cloth, printed in blue

Stein, Gertrude. Portrait of Mabel Dodge at the Villa Curonia. (Florence, 1912). 12: imprint at bottom

Stein, Gertrude. Prothalamium. [Culver, Indiana, 1939]. FC: [ornament] *Prothalamium| for| Bobolink and his Louisa| a poem| Gertrude Stein*

Steinbeck, John. America and Americans. NY, (1966). B: lettering runs down spine

Steinbeck, John. Cannery Row. NY, 1945. B: off-white, cream cloth (second issue: yellow; much later reprint: blue)

Steinbeck, John. East of Eden. NY, 1952. 281.38: *bite*

Steinbeck, John. The Grapes of Wrath. NY, (1939). DJ: front flap: *First Edition* on lower inner corner

Steinbeck, John. The Moon is Down. NY. 1942. CP: no printer's name   112.11: *talk.this*   DJ: sharp, square corners only on all four flaps, not clipped at an angle

Steinbeck, John. Of Mice and Men. NY, (1937). 9.2-3 up: *and only moved because the heavy hands were / pendula.*

Steinbeck, John. The Pastures of Heaven. NY, 1932. IM: *Brewer, Warren & Putnam*

Steinbeck, John. The Pearl. NY, 1947. DJ: photo of Steinbeck looking to his left, printing is black

Steinbeck, John. A Russian Journal. NY, 1958. B: grey-green cloth   SP: grey-yellowish brown

Steinbeck, John. Sweet Thursday. NY, 1954. B: beige cloth   TE: red   TP: printed in red & black   CP: printer's name   BC: no book club deboss at lower corner near spine   DJ: back cover: no blurbs beneath photo of Steinbeck

Steinbeck, John. To a God Unknown. NY, (1933). IM: *Robert O. Ballou*

Steinbeck, John. Travels with Charley in Search of America. NY, (1962). DJ: no mention of Nobel Prize

Simic, Charles. What the Grass Says. (Santa Cruz, 1967).
　　B: blue grey wrappers　ST: dark brown & yellow-gold
　　EP: Colophon present
Sinclair, Upton. The Brass Check. Pasadena, 1919.
　　Last p. is 444, no notes
Sinclair, Upton. The Jungle. NY, 1906. SP: *Jungle Publishing Co.*
　　FC: Atlas seal　Slip: *Sustainer's Edition* pasted in
Sinjohn, John. *See* **Galsworthy, John.**
Siringo, Charles A. A Cowboy Detective. C, 1912.　IM: *Conkey*
Siringo, Charles A. Riati and Spurs. B, 1927.　TP: *1927*
Sitwell, Edith. I Live Under a Black Sun. L, 1937.
　　B: black cloth with buff stamping
Sitwell, Sacheverell. Conversation Pieces. L, (1936).
　　B: vii-viii: integral
Sitwell, Sacheverell. Edinburgh. L, (1938). B: lilac cloth boards
Sitwell, Sacheverell. The Romantic Ballet in Lithographs of the Time. L, (1938).
　　B: rose pink silk cloth boards with fleur-de-lys pattern
Smith, Clark Ashton. The Startreaders. SF, 1912.
　　B: white　DJ: white stamped in gilt
Smith, F. Hopkinson. Colonel Carter of Cartersville. B, 1891.
　　1: picture of staircase　ADS: no mention of this title
Smith, Logan Pearsall. The Youth of Parnassus and Other Stories. L, 1895.　B: blue cloth
Smith, Martin Cruz. Nightwing. NY, (1977).
　　BC: no book club deboss at lower corner near spine
Southern, Terry. Flash & Filigree. NY, (1958).
　　DJ: *$3.00*　B: Full cloth
Spender, Stephen. The Burning Cactus. L, 1936.
　　First and last leaves blank
Steichen, Edward. A Life in Photography. NY, 1963.
　　EP: patterned photo of tacks　PA: text on dull non-coated; photos dull coated　B: dull cloth
Stein, Gertrude. An Acquaintance with Description. L, 1929.
　　36.2: *mnay*
Stein, Gertrude. Autobiography of Alice B. Toklas. NY, (1933). DJ: no printed price　B: silver-blue cloth
　　EP: white　ST: silver on cover & spine

Boyd, James. Roll River. NY, 1935. 364.3 up: *senitmental*
Boyle, Kay. Breaking the Silence. NY, (1962).
　　WR: *September, 1962* on back
Bradbury, Ray. The Day It Rained Forever. L, 1959.
　　B: medium blue
Bradbury, Ray. Death is a Lonely Business. NY, 1985.
　　DJ: *$16.95 ($15.95* is second issue)
Bradbury, Ray. The Last Circus and the Electrocution. Northridge, CA, 1980. DJ: red on yellow
Bradbury, Ray. The Martian Chronicles. GC, 1950. B: green
Bradbury, Ray. The October Country. NY, (1955).
　　SP: Ballantine logo upside down
Bradbury, Ray. S is for Space. GC, 1966. (238): *H27*　Also, Library Edition: (139): *H27*
Bradbury, Ray. Switch on the Night. (NY, 1963).　Library edition: pictorial cover　BC: library edition definition
Bradbury, Ray. Twice 22. GC, 1966. TP: *1966*　CP: no usual Doubleday *First Edition*　405: *47g*
Brand, Millen. The Outward Room. NY, 1937. DJ: pictorial & with no blurbs by Theodore Dreiser and Fannie Hurst
Brautigan, Richard. The Confederate General From Big Sur. NY, (1964).　CP: No usual Grove Press *First Printing*
Brooks, Gwendolyn. Bronzeville Boys and Girls. NY, (1956).　CP: no usual Harper *First Edition*
Brooks, Gwendolyn. Riot. Detroit, (1969). 22: *these*
Brooks, Gwendolyn. The World of Gwendolyn Brooks. NY, (1971). Last p.: *1*　DJ: flap: *0971*
Browning, Elizabeth Barrett. The Greek Christian Poets. L, 1863. 205.16-17: *...all ...full*
Browning, Elizabeth Barrett. Poems. L, 1850.
　　TP: *Chapman & Hall, 186, Strand*
Browning, Elizabeth Barrett. Prometheus Bound. L, 1833. 154.13: *tongues, that*
Buck, Pearl S. The Good Earth. NY, (1931).　TE: brown　CP: *For the John Day Publishing Company, Inc.*　100.17: *flees*
Bukowski, Charles. The Days Run Away Like Wild Horses Over the Hills. Los Angeles, 1969. Wraps. 19.15: *1943*
Burgess, Gelett. The Purple Cow! (SF, 1895).
　　PA: printed on both sides of the leaves

Burnett, Frances Hodgson. A Lady of Quality. NY, 1896.
    p.(-)2v lists 17 entries, the first is *That Lass o' Lowrie's*
Burnett, Frances Hodgson. Little Lord Fauntleroy. NY,
    1886. IM: *De Vinne* on page 210
Burnett, Frances Hodgson. Surly Tim and Other Stories.
    NY, 1877. (274): blank
Burroughs, Edgar Rice. A Fighting Man of Mars. NY, 1931.
    TP: *Metropolitan Books*
Burroughs, Edgar Rice. Tarzan of the Apes. C, 1914. SP:
    acorn-shaped device CP: printer's name in Old English
Burroughs, Edgar Rice. Tarzan of the Apes. L, (1917).
    ADS: *Autumn*
Burroughs, John. Leaf and Tendril. B and NY, 1908.
    SP: *Houghton/Mifflin & Co.*
**Burroughs, John. Notes on Walt Whitman as Poet and
    Person.** NY, 1867. PA: leaves trimmed to 6 9/16" tall
Burroughs, William. The Naked Lunch. NY, (1962).
    DJ: back panel: no zip code; no roman numerals on
    lower spine near back panel
Burroughs, William. The Naked Lunch. Paris, 1959.
    WR: green preferred, decorated also of value; price on
    back: *Francs 1,500*
Burroughs, William. So Who Owns Death TV? n.p., n.d.
    IFC: *50c*
Butler, Samuel. Erewhon Revisited Twenty Years Later.
    L, 1901. Preface: errata slip
Byrne, Donn. Blind Raftery and His Wife Hilaria. NY,
    (1924). 108.last: perfect type 138.: perfect type
Byrne, Donn. Crusade. B, 1928. 250: integral, not a cancel
    Probable error in date
Byrne, Donn. The Lyric Year. One Hundred Poems. NY,
    1912. 25.7up: *careful gentlemen*
Byrne, Donn. Messer Marco Polo. NY, 1921. 10.last: *of* perfect
    10.last: *forgettng* 145-6 is end paper
Byrne, Donn. The Wind Bloweth. NY, 1922.
    151.9up: *mouth of money*
Byron, George Gordon (Lord). The Bride of Abydos. L,
    1813. errata slip present

**Shaw, George Bernard. John Bull's Other Island and Major
    Barbara.** L, 1907. TP: *Archibald Constable & Co. Ltd.*
    SP: publisher's imprint
Shaw, George Bernard. Love Among the Artists. L, 1914.
    B: green cloth SP: gilt stamping
Shaw, George Bernard. The Matter With Ireland. L, 1962.
    B: rust-red cloth TE: rust stained FC: double-rule at top
    and *Hart-Davis* are 0.3cm from edge
Shaw, George Bernard. On Language. NY, (1963).
    B: black cloth with pale blue stamping
Shaw, George Bernard. The Perfect Wagnerite. L, 1898.
    B: blue-ribbed quarter cloth, linen sides
Shaw, George Bernard. Press Cuttings. L, 1909.
    B: blue flecked, pink paper wrappers TP: *Archibald
    Constable & Co.* FC: *Price One Shilling*
**Shaw, George Bernard. Pygmalion: a Romance in Five
    Acts.** L, 1913. TP: *Rough Proof, Unpublished*
Shaw, George Bernard. The Quintessence of G.B.S.
    L, (1949). B: blue cloth
Shaw, George Bernard. The Quintessence of Ibsenism.
    L, 1891. B: dark blue cloth
Shaw, George Bernard. Ruskin's Politics. Oxford, 1921.
    Label: *G. Bernard Shaw*
Shaw, George Bernard. Saint Joan: a Chronicle Play.
    L, 1923. TP: *Rough Proof, Unpublished*
Shaw, George Bernard. Selected Passages. NY, 1913.
    B: maroon limp leather
Shaw, George Bernard. Shaw on Shakespeare. NY, 1961.
    WR: white, stiff paper
**Shaw, George Bernard. Spoken English and Broken
    English.** L, (1928). WR: addresses of 12 foreign
    branches of Linguaphone Institute present
Shaw, George Bernard. An Unsocial Socialist. L, 1887.
    TP: *Author of "The Confessions of Byron Cashel's Profession,"
    etc., etc.* SP: *Sonnenschein* in gilt B: red cloth
Shiel, M.P. Prince Zaleski. L, 1895.
    Back of book: 16 page catalog
Sidney, Margaret. Five Little Peppers and How They Grew.
    B, (1880). 231.caption: *said Polly*

Saroyan, William. **The Human Comedy.** NY, (1943).
>DJ: front flap: box "*Send this book...*" at bottom under address; back flap: *$2.50* price; back panel: no box: "*The Men in the Services Need Books!*" etc.

Sarton, May. **Kinds of Love.** NY, (1970).
>DJ: front flap: no reviews

Sassoon, Siegfried. **Memoirs of a Fox-Hunting Man.** L, (1928). Fore edges: trimmed

Sassoon, Siegfried. **Memoirs of an Infantry Officer.** L, (1920).
>E: untrimmed

Schwartz, Delmore. **I am Cherry Alive, the Little Girl Sang.** NY, (1979). No statement of first edition, as is usual with this publisher

Schwartz, Delmore. **The World is a Wedding.** (Norfolk, Conn., 1948). B: grey cloth ST: green

Scott, Walter. **Goetz of Berlichingen With the Iron Hand.** L, 1799. TP: *William Scott, Esq.*

Scott, Walter. **The Heart of Midlothian. Tales of My Landlord, Second Series.** 4 vols. Edinburgh, 1818.
>Vol 1: p.1: no volume number or signature at foot

Scott, Walter. **Redgauntlet, a Tale of the Eighteenth Century.** 3 vols. Edinburgh, 1824. HT: none

Sendak, Maurice (illustrator). Eidinoff & Ruchlis. **Atomics for the Millions.** NY, (1947).
>CP: statement on paper quality

Seton, Ernest Thompson. **Wild Animals I Have Known.** NY, 1898.
>265.last paragraph: *The Angel whispered don't go* absent

Shaw, George Bernard. **Cashel Byron's Profession.** C, 1901.
>B: chocolate brown cloth

Shaw, George Bernard. **Fabian Election Manifesto.** (n.p.), 1892. 16: no printer's imprint and no committee list

Shaw, George Bernard. **Fabian Essays in Socialism.** L, 1889.
>FC: *1889*

Shaw, George Bernard. **Geneva, Cymbeline Refinished & Good King Charles.** L, (1947). TE: gilt

Shaw, George Bernard. **How To Settle the Irish Question.** Dublin, (1917). B: blue paper wrappers

Byron, George Gordon (Lord). **The Prisoner of Chillon, and Other Poems.** L, 1816. PA: recto of E8 is blank

Cabell, James Branch. **Beyond Life.** NY, 1919.
>B: very dark brown cloth TP: no accent in *Demiurges*

Cabell, James Branch. **The Certain Hour.** NY, 1917.
>B: no kalki stamp

Cabell, James Branch. **Chivalry.** NY, 1909.
>B: red ST: green & white L: gilt

Cabell, James Branch. **The Cords of Vanity.** NY, 1909.
>SP: *Cords of Vanity*, no *The* FC: *Cords of Vanity*; no *The*

Cabell, James Branch. **The Cream of the Jest.** NY, 1917.
>FC: no kalki stamp

Cabell, James Branch. **The Eagle's Shadow.** NY, 1904.
>DP: *To M.L.P.B.*
>FP: seated figure; quotation marks in caption imperfect

Cabell, James Branch. **Figures of Earth.** NY, 1925. CP: *First Printing of Illustrated Edition December, 1925* not present

Cabell, James Branch. **From the Hidden Way.** NY, 1916.
>Edges: trimmed SP: no dash under *c* in *McBride*

Cabell, James Branch. **Gallantry.** NY, 1907.
>B: grey cloth ST: white & silver L: gilt

Cabell, James Branch. **Jurgen.** NY, 1919.
>Across top of covers: 1 1/4" 144: line rules perfect

Cabell, James Branch. **The Line of Love.** NY, 1905.
>ST: white and gilt

Cabell, James Branch. **The Music From Behind the Moon.** NY, 1926. SP: label 3/8" wide

Cabell, James Branch. **The Soul of Melicent.** NY, (1913).
>B: dark blue cloth

Cabell, James Branch. **These Restless Heads.** NY, 1932.
>1st trade CP: *Second Printing*

Cable, George W. **The Busy Man's Bible and How to Study and Teach** It. Meadville, PA, 1891.
>IM: *Penna* 20.2up: *genuing* 33.5: *dilligence*

Cable, George W. **The Cavalier.** NY, 1901. FC: black sword & wing design; gilt stamping & ornament

Cable, George W. **John March Southerner.** NY, 1894. B: green cloth FC: black sword & wing with gilt ornament

Cable, George W. Kincaid's Battery. NY, 1908.
  B: stamped in color & gilt   CP: *Caxton Press*
Cable, George W. Old Creole Days. NY, 1879. ADS: not present
Cahan, A. Yekl. A Tale of the New York Ghetto. NY, 1896.
  ADS: 12 p. at back, undated, and no mention of this title
Calisher, Hortense. Herself. NY, (1972).
  DJ: back panel: *On Women*
Camus, Albert. Resistance, Rebellion, and Death. NY, 1961. DJ: front flap: no Charles Rolo quote; back flap: no type between *New York* and *Printed in U.S.A.*
Capote, Truman. A Christmas Memory. NY, (1956).
  CP: no usual Random House *First Printing*
Capote, Truman. The Grass Harp. (NY, 1951).
  B: rough beige linen
Capote, Truman. The Grass Harp (play). (NY, 1954).
  First revised edition. BC: first new title: *Inherit the Wind*
Capote, Truman. House of Flowers. NY, (1968).
  CP: no usual Random House *First Printing*
Capote, Truman. In Cold Blood. NY, (1965).
  DJ: front flap: *1/66*; back flap: *Publishers of the American College Dictionary and the Modern Library*
Caputo, Philip. Rumor of War. NY, (1977).
  BC: no book club deboss at lower corner near spine
Carman, Bliss. Behind the Arras: A Book of the Unseen. B, 1895. IM: no *Briggs* or *Mathews*
Carman, Bliss. Echoes from Vagabondia. B, 1912.
  FC: *Hovey* as co-author
Carman, Bliss. Low Tide on Grand Pre. T, (1889 or '90).
  Author's name: *Carmen*
Carman, Bliss. The Vengeance of Noel Brassard.
  Cambridge, 1919 (actually 1899). TP: *MDCCCCXIX*
Carr, John Dickson. The Dead Man's Knock. NY, (1958).
  B: blue & black cloth   CP: *G-H*
Carroll, Lewis. An Easter Greeting to Every Child Who Loves "Alice." [Easter, 1876].
  P: watermarked *E. Towgood Fine*
Carroll, Lewis. Sylvie and Bruno Concluded. L, 1893.
  Table of Contents: *Chapter 8* given as *p. 110*

Roosevelt, Theodore. Ranch Life and the Hunting-Trail. NY, (1888). E: all gilt B: light, coarse weave, tan buckram FC: stamped in green and gilt
Roosevelt, Theodore. The Ship of State. B, 1903.
  B: blue cloth FC: full-rigged ship in green, title orange SP: stamping gilt
Roosevelt, Theodore. The Strenuous Life. NY, 1900.
  225 pages only
Roosevelt, Theodore. The Wilderness Hunter. NY, (1893).
  Chapter heads: brown
Roosevelt, Theodore. The Winning of the West. NY, 1889-96.
  4 vols. Vol. I, 160.last: *diame-* 161.first: *ter*
Salinger, J.D. The Catcher in the Rye. B, 1951. DJ: back panel: photo of author by Lotte Jacobi; front flap: price (not Book-of-the-Month Club slug)
Salinger, J.D. Raise High the Roof Beam, Carpenters, and Seymour: An Introduction. B, (1959). DP: none (DP in varying locations, tipped or bound in, in later issues)
Saltus, Edgar. Daughters of the Rich. NY, 1909.
  IM: *Mitchell Kennerly*
Saltus, Edgar. The Lords of the Ghostland. NY, 1907.
  TE: gilt Page size: 7 1/4" tall TP: stamping red
Saltus, Edgar. Mr. Incoul's Misadventure. NY, 1887.
  EP: green No ads for *Sea Spray*
Saltus, Edgar. A Transient Guest and Other Episodes. C, (1889). SP: *Belford Clarke & Co.*
  CP: *Press of E.B. Sheldon & Co.*
Saltus, Edgar. The Truth About Tristrem Varick. C, (1888).
  SP: *Belford Clarke & Co.*
Saltus, Edgar. Vanity Square. Ph, 1906.
  FC: pictorial B: has head and tail bands
Sandburg, Carl. Abraham Lincoln: the Prairie Years. NY, (1926). 2 vols. Large paper ed.: Vol. I, 174.9: *ears*
Sandburg, Carl. Chicago Poems. NY, 1916. ADS: p.1: *3'16*
Sandburg, Carl. Cornhuskers. NY, 1918. 3: so numbered TP: book list opposite gives *$1.30* price for *Chicago Poems*
Sandburg, Carl. Slabs of the Sunburnt West. NY, (1922).
  75 is last P. of text

Riley, James Whitcomb. Poems Here at Home. NY, 1893.
   [2]: *Neighborly* 50.5.1st stanza: *girls*
Riley, James Whitcomb. Rhymes of Childhood. Ind, 1891.
   FC: child's head design   64.12: *sometimes*
Riley, James Whitcomb. Riley Love-Lyrics. Ind, (1899).
   IM: *Bowen-Merrill*
   xvi: *The Passing of a Heart* listed as being on p. *71*
Riley, James Whitcomb. While the Heart Beats Young. Ind, (1906). Table of Contents: all but two poems listed two pages short of actual appearance
Roberts, Elizabeth Madox. The Time of Man. NY, 1926.
   TP: title in dark blue
Roberts, Kenneth. Arundel. GC, 1930. 28.35: *them*
   84.6: *had*   196.1: *protected*   299.17: *chokecheeries*
Roberts, Kenneth. Europe's Morning After. NY,(1921).CP: *B-V*
Roberts, Kenneth. Sun Hunting. Ind, (1922).
   B: green cloth   ST: gilt
Robinson, Edwin Arlington. Lancelot. NY, 1920. B: green
Robinson, Edwin Arlington. The Man Against the Sky. NY, 1916.   TE: gilt
Robinson, Edwin Arlington. Matthias at the Door. NY, 1931.
   97.5 up : no punctuation at end
Robinson, Edwin Arlington. Merlin. NY, 1917.
   79.8: *...with only philosophy*
Robinson, Edwin Arlington. The Porcupine. NY, 1915. TE: gilt   FC: rules and stamping gilt   2-3: erratum slip
Robinson, Edwin Arlington. Tristram. NY, 1927. 86.2: *rocks*
Robinson, Edwin Arlington. Van Zorn. NY, 1914.
   TE: gilt   FC: rules and stamping gilt
Robinson, Rowland E. Hunting Without a Gun. NY, 1905.
   SP: *Forest and stream*
Roosevelt, Theodore. Fear God and Take Your Own Part. NY, (1916). B: red cloth
Roosevelt, Theodore. The Foes of Our Own Household. NY, (1917). TP: printer's monogram 3/8" diameter
Roosevelt, Theodore. Letters to His Children. NY, 1919.
   3.3: *twenty*

Carroll, Lewis. Symbolic Logic. L, 1896.
   Errata slip, dated *Feb. 24, 1896*, precedes p. 1 of text
Carroll, Lewis. Through the Looking Glass. L,1872. 21:2: *wade*
Cary, Joyce. The Horse's Mouth. NY, (1944). BC: no deboss at lower right corner   DJ: front flap: *No. 7768*   back flap: *No. 7769*; back panel: *No. 3170*
Cather, Willa. Alexander's Bridge. B, 1912. SP: Willa S. Cather   B: blue or lavender mesh cloth   ST: gilt   HT: precedes TP & has author's name & title in box
Cather, Willa. Death Comes for the Archbishop. NY, 1927.
   CP: Copyright 1926, 1927   TE: stained ochre
   EP: cream wove stock
Cather, Willa. A Lost Lady. NY, 1923. B: green cloth   ST: gilt
   CP: 1st trade: *First and Second Printings Before Publication Published September, 1923*   174.19: *of* correctly printed
Cather, Willa. My Antonia. B, 1918. IL: glazed paper & inserted
Cather, Willa writing as **S. S. McClure. My Autobiography.**
   NY, (1914). CP: *May, 1914*   Leaf 16-17: integral
   239.13: *H.H. Rogers for his comment and suggestions*
Cather, Willa. O Pioneers! B, 1913. B: light yellow-brown or pale cream yellow vertical ribbed cloth   ST: the period after Co. in *Houghton Mifflin Co.* touches the *o*
   Final leaf: (21/1) is tipped in
Cather, Willa. The Professor's House. NY, 1925.   CP: *Copyright 1925, By Willa Cather*   B: orange linen cloth
Cather, Willa. Sapphira and the Slave Girl. NY, 1940.
   DJ: back panel: *BORZOI BOOKS* logo at bottom
Cather, Willa. Shadows on the Rock. NY, 1931.
   CP: *SECOND EDITION*   250.18: *hay-bale*
Cather, Willa. The Song of the Lark. B, 1915.
   CP: ADS in box; titles by Cather   8.3up: *moment*
Cather, Willa. The Troll Garden. NY, 1905.
   SP: *McClure Phillips & Co.*
Chambers, Robert W. Cardigan. NY, 1901. 213: so numbered
Chambers, Robert W. The Maid at Arms. NY,1902. IM: *Harper*
Chandler, Raymond. Chandler Before Marlowe. Columbia, (1973). CP: *Second Printing, July 1973*
Charteris, Leslie. Featuring the Saint. L, (1931). B: red covers

Chatwin, Bruce. In Patagonia. L, (1977).
    EP: blue & white, decorated with map
Chatwin, Bruce. On the Black Hill. L, (1982).
    DJ: *7.50* pounds
Chatwin, Bruce. The Songlines. L, (1987).
    DJ: no reviews of this title
Cheever, John. The Brigadier and the Golf Widow. NY, 1964. DJ: back panel: author's photo, not reviews
Cheever, John. The Enormous Radio & Other Stories. NY, 1953. DJ: front flap: *$3.50* ; back panel: photo of author with cigarette & ashtray with curtain backdrop
Chestnutt, Charles Waddell. The Colonel's Dream. NY, 1905. FC: *Chestnutt* SP: *Chestnutt*
Chesterton, G.K. The Turkey and the Turk. Ditchling, (1930).
    B: morocco-backed, fine-grained light green cloth
    DJ: yellow with repro of IL on p.9 in black
Christie, Agatha. Easy to Kill. NY, 1939. DJ: *$2.00*
Christie, Agatha. Toward Zero. NY, 1944.
    TP: no *Distributed by Blakiston*
Churchill, Winston. The Crisis. NY, 1901. 257.38: *its head*
Churchill, Winston S. Arms and the Covenant. L, (1938).
    DJ: red on yellow
Churchill, Winston S. Blood, Sweat and Tears. T, (1941).
    B: lacks speech *War With Germany*
Churchill, Winston S. Blood, Sweat and Tears. NY, (1941).
    B: blue cloth TE: stained red
Churchill, Winston S. A History of the English-Speaking Peoples. 4 vols. Volume II. The New World. NY, (1956). B: light to medium red panels on spine, bulking 42mm BC: no book club deboss at lower corner near spine DJ: price present
Churchill, Winston S. In the Balance - Speeches 1949 and 1950. L, (1951). B: first gathering bound so that last leaf of contents appears prior to half-title
Churchill, Winston S. Into Battle. L, (1941). PA: no leaf numbered *128 a/b* attached to 5v of Section 1 with speech *War on Germany*

Richards, Laura E. Captain January. B, 1891.
    CP: presswork and typography note
Richter, Conrad. Brothers of No Kin and Other Stories. NY, (c. 1942). DJ: white
Riley, James Whitcomb. Afterwhiles. Ind, 1888. 27.4up: *and*
Riley, James Whitcomb. Armazindy. Ind, 1894. FP: inserted, no other illustrations in book ii: so numbered Contents on vii-viii 110: 26 lines deep No ads
Riley, James Whitcomb. The Boys of the Old Glee Club. Ind, (1907). B: light yellow-green CP: *November*
Riley, James Whitcomb. Character Sketches, The Boss Girl, A Christmas Story, and Other Sketches. Ind, 1886. CP: *Riley* in copyright notice 9.5: *stir!*
Riley, James Whitcomb. A Child-World. Ind, 1897.
    [ix]: Proem [xv]: half-title
Riley, James Whitcomb. The Flying Islands of the Night. Ind, 1892. B: white flexible boards
Riley, James Whitcomb. Green Fields and Running Brooks. Ind, 1893. 16.1: *miles on miles*
Riley, James Whitcomb. His Pa's Romance. Ind, (1903).
    CP: *November*
Riley, James Whitcomb. Home-Folks. Ind, (1900).
    59: heading repeated
Riley, James Whitcomb. The Lockerbie Book. Ind, (1911).
    617-630: titles indexed by page
Riley, James Whitcomb. Morning. Ind, (1907).
    [ii]: *Neghborly Poems* CP: *October*
Riley, James Whitcomb. Neghborly Poems. Ind, 1891.
    CP: *1891* only [ii]: no mention of "*The Flying Islands of the Night*" or "*An Old Sweetheart of Mine*"
Riley, James Whitcomb. Nye and Riley's Railway Guide.
    C, 1888. B: [1-14] 8, wire stitched
Riley, James Whitcomb. An Old Sweetheart of Mine.
    Ind, (1902). EP: black stamping B: signatures in 8
Riley, James Whitcomb. Out to Old Aunt Mary's. Ind, (1904).
    PROEM text is 1 5/8" 2nd stanza.3: *... cherry ...*
Riley, James Whitcomb. Pipes O'Pan at Zekesbury. Ind, 1889. PA: wove 79.1.3rd stanza: *farmer* CP: printer's slug

Pyle, Howard. **Ruby of Kishmoor.** NY, 1908.
  B: slate green cloth ST: gilt IM: *jolly roger*
Pyle, Howard. **Within the Capes.** NY, 1885. B: cloth
Pynchon, Thomas. **Entropy.** (Troy Town, England, 1967 [actually 1981]). B: green wrappers, black stamping
Pynchon, Thomas. **Gravity's Rainbow.** NY, (1973).
  DJ: *$15.00* and; BC: ISBN printed in white over red
Pynchon, Thomas. **Morality and Mercy in Vienna.** (L, 1970).
  B: smooth white wrappers
Pynchon, Thomas. **V.** Ph, (1963). CP: no usual Lippincott statement *FIRST EDITION* DJ: no reviews on back
Rackham, Arthur. **The Allies' Fairy Book.** L, 1916.
  EP: pictorial
Rackham, Arthur. **Mother Goose; The Old Nursery Rhymes.** L, 1913. EP: pictorial
Rand, Ayn. **Anthem.** L, (1938). DJ: SP: *6s Net*
Rand, Ayn. **Atlas Shrugged.** NY, (1957). DJ: front flap: *10/57*; back flap: publisher's name and address present
Rand, Ayn. **The Fountainhead.** Ind, (1943).
  B: red cloth DJ: *$3.00* with Bobbs-Merrill titles on back
Rand, Ayn. **Philosophy: Who Needs It.** Ind/NY, (1982).
  CP: first two lines of copyright notice stamped
Rand, Ayn. **The Virtue of Selfishness, A New Concept of Egoism.** (NY, 1964). B: no business reply card bound in
Remington, Frederic. **Done in the Open.** NY, 1902.
  FC: *Frederick* 9: so numbered
Remington, Frederic. **Men with the Bark On.** NY, 1900.
  Across top of covers: 7/8"
Remington, Frederic. **The Way of an Indian.** NY, 1906.
  ST: yellow SP: *Fox Duffield & Company*
Rhys, Jean. **After Leaving Mr. Mackenzie.** NY, (1931 [actually 1972]). CP: no *First Edition* as is usual (192): 7273 10987654321
Rhys, Jean. **The Left Bank and Other Stories.** NY, (1927).
  No *First Edition* as is usual; reason: English sheets with cancel title page
Rice, Alice Hegan. *See* **Hegan, Alice.**
Rice, Anne. **Memnoch the Devil.** NY, 1995.
  Back cover of DJ must have *52500* on bar code

Churchill, Winston S. **Marlborough His Life and Times.** L, (1933). V. I: errata slip tipped-in between (16)-17
  V. II: errata slip tipped-in facing 434
  V. III: errata slip tipped-in facing (18)
Churchill, Winston S. **Marlborough His Life and Times.** NY, 1933. Vol V: errata slip tipped-in between (18)-19
Churchill, Winston S. **My African Journey.** L, 1908.
  B: Red pictorial cloth
Churchill, Winston S. **My Early Life.** L, (1930).
  Verso of half-title: *The World Crisis* not listed
Churchill, Winston S. **The People's Rights.** L, (1910).
  B: index present
Churchill, Winston S. **Savrola.** NY, 1900. B: dark blue cloth
Churchill, Winston S. **The Second World War.** B, 1948.
  TE: yellow-brown B: red cloth with red and yellow imitation head- and footbands
Churchill, Winston S. **The Story of the Malakand Field Force. . .** L, 1898. ADS: none   No errata slip tipped in following first folding map
Churchill, Winston S. **The World Crisis.** L, 1923.
  Vol I: errata slip tipped-in between (vi)-I Vol IV: errata slip tipped-in between pages 10-11
Clancy, Tom. **The Hunt for Red October.** Annapolis, (1984).
  CP: no statement of edition; no series of numbers
  DJ: no price
Clavell, James. **Whirlwind.** NY, (1986). Two states: Canadian: *FPu (1986) w/N* and U.S.: *FE w/N*; other info on CPs differ substantially; DJs are identical
Clemens, Samuel Langhorne. *See* **Twain, Mark.**
Cobb, Irvin S. **Back Home.** NY, (1912).
  CP: *Plimpton Press*; publisher's name in three lines
  Text: pages: 2 rules above, 1 below text
Cobb, Irvin S. **Down Yonder with Judge Priest and Irvin S. Cobb.** NY, 1932. 251.11: *quarel*
Cobb, Irvin S. **Old Judge Priest.** NY, (1916).
  DP: *Margaret Mayo Selwyn*
Conrad, Joseph. **Almayer's Folly.** L, 1895.
  110.2up: *g nerosity* 110.2up *of* omitted

Conrad, Joseph. Almayer's Folly. NY, 1895. B: dark blue smooth cloth SP: *Macmillan & Co.*
Conrad, Joseph. Chance. L, (1914). CP: *First published in 1913*
Conrad, Joseph. Chance. NY, 1913. TP: *1913* & publisher's device
Conrad, Joseph. The Children of the Sea. NY, 1897. CP: *Copyright, 1897, by...*
Conrad, Joseph. The Dover Patrol. Canterbury, 1922. TP: *L* absent
Conrad, Joseph. The Inheritors. NY, 1901. DP: *To Boys and Christina*
Conrad, Joseph. The Inheritors. L, 1901. B: 189 x 127mm, smooth yellow cloth TE: untrimmed ADS: 32 pp.
Conrad, Joseph. Lord Jim. NY, 1900. CP: *Copyright, 1900 / By Doubleday, Page & Co...*
Conrad, Joseph. The Mirror of the Sea. L, 1906. ADS: 40 pages, dated *July* or *August, 1906*
Conrad, Joseph. The Nigger of the "Narcissus." L, 1898. B: slate colored cloth SP: *H* in *Heinemann* is 5.5mm tall, other letters 4mm ADS: at end, *Mr. William Heinemann's / Autumn Announcements / mdcccxcvii*
Conrad, Joseph. Notes on Life and Letters. L, 1921. iv: no PRIVATELY PRINTED   xi; Table of Contents: *S* and *a* missing from *Tales of the Sea*
Conrad, Joseph. The Point of Honor. NY, 1908. SP: *McClure*
Conrad, Joseph. The Secret Agent. L, (1907). ADS: *September*
Conrad, Joseph: The Secret Agent: a Drama in Three Acts. L, 1923. 117: *anarchist activity was to be be apprehended.*
Conrad, Joseph. A Set of Six. L, 1908. ADS: *February, 1908* HT: no *Methuen's Colonial Library*
Conrad, Joseph. 'Twixt Land and Sea, Tales. L, 1912. B: green vertically-ribbed cloth FC: *Freya of the Secret Isles*
Conrad, Joseph. Typhoon. L, 1903. TE: only edge trimmed SP: top of Heinemann to bottom of Conrad 110mm TP: windmill symbol and *Reserved for the Colonies only* absent iii, series halftitle: *Heinemann's Colonial Library...* ADS: 32 pp. at end
Conrad, Joseph. Typhoon. NY, 1902. ADS: 4 pages

Pound, Ezra. Provenca: Poems Selected from "Personae," "Exultations," and "Canzoniere." B, (1910). ST: dark brown; title measures 9cm B: stamped in dark brown
Pound, Ezra. A Quinzaine for This Yule. (L, 1908). 17.5: *earth-board's* 18.3: *earth-board's* 21.6: *Weston St. Llewmy*
Pound, Ezra. The Spirit of Romance. W.C. (1910). B: olive brown cloth boards TE: gilt, others untrimmed
Pound, Ezra. Thrones. (NY, 1959). 85.9: *no war*
Powers, J. F. Prince of Darkness. GC, 1947. DJ: ads on back panel include *Prince of Darkness* Later DJ: critical reviews
Powys, John. Corinth. (Oxford, 1891). FC: *English Verse* End of text: author's name present
Powys, Theodore Francis. Black Byrony. L, 1923. B: light grey mottled cloth TE: green
Powys, Theodore Francis. Soliloquies of a Hermit. L, 1918. B: light blue boards
Price, Reynolds. Early Dark, a Play. NY, 1977. DJ: SP: author's name not present
Price, Reynolds. The Good News According to Mark. n.p., 1976. EP: dark orange
Price, Reynolds. A Long and Happy Life. NY, 1962. DJ: *Stephen Spender, Lord David Cecil, Francis Gray Patton, Harper Lee* & the dashes before their names & *Jacket design: Janet Halverson* in pale yellowish green
Price, Reynolds. Two Theophanies. (Durham, 1971). WR: purple with silver ink
Proulx, Annie. The Shipping News. NY, (1993). FF: DJ: rear flap: *Printed in USA*
Purdy, James. Malcolm. NY, (1959). No statement of first edition as is usual with this publisher
Pyle, Howard. Howard Pyle's Book of Pirates. NY, 1912. CP: *D-V*
Pyle, Howard. Howard Pyle's Book of the American Spirit. NY, 1923. CP: *B-X*
Pyle, Howard. Men of Iron. NY, 1892. Across top of covers: 1 1/16"
Pyle, Howard. The Price of Blood. B, 1899. B: boards, cloth back SP: no lettering

Porter, Katherine Anne. The Days Before. NY, (1952).
  DJ: back flap: no statement beginning *The Jacket portrait of Katherine Anne Porter...*
Porter, Katherine Anne. Flowering Judas and Other Stories. NY, (1935). CP: publisher's ornament present
Porter, Katherine Anne. Flowering Judas and Other Stories. NY, (1940). First Modern Library edition. DJ: back panel: *20 East 57th Street.*
Porter, Katherine Anne. Flowering Judas and Other Stories. NY, (1935). First expanded edition. DJ: dark green and brown   CP: copyright notice in name of *Harcourt, Brace and Company, Inc.*
Porter, Katherine Anne. Hacienda. (NY, 1934). 52.16: *up to his middle in the cold water of the horse* 52-3: No erratum slip
Porter, Katherine Anne. My Chinese Marriage by M.T.F. NY, 1921. TP: *1921*
Porter, Katherine Anne. The Old Order. NY, (1955). CP: no printing code [B,C, etc.]; no usual Harcourt *first edition*
Post, Melville Davisson. Monsieur Jonquelle. NY, 1923.
  B: 62 and 63 reversed
Potter, Beatrix. The Tale of Peter Rabbit. L, 1902.
  First trade edition. EP: holly leaf design 51: *wept*
Pound, Ezra. Cantos LII-LXXI. L, (1940). DJ: front flap: *10s.6d*
Pound, Ezra. Canzoni. L, (1911). B: streaky grey cloth boards
Pound, Ezra. A Draft of XXX Cantos. NY, (1933). 62:11up: *shit*
Pound, Ezra. The Fourth Canto. (L), 1919.
  Col: *by John Rodker. Completed*
Pound, Ezra. Gaudier=Brzeska. L/NY, 1916. B: approximately 200 sets of sheets in grey-green cloth boards embossed in blind with reproduction of a green stone charm on FC
Pound, Ezra. Gold and Labour. L, 1951. 11.40-41: reference to Churchill, Roosevelt & Baruch 14.6: uncomplimentary description of Philip Gibbs
Pound, Ezra. Make It New. L, (1934). DJ: front flap: *12s.6d*
Pound, Ezra. Pavannes and Divisions. NY, 1918. B: dark blue cloth boards ST: blind on both covers, gilt on spine
Pound, Ezra. Personae, Collected Poems of. NY, (1949).
  DJ: no ad for *"Section: Rock-Drill"*

Conrad, Joseph. Under Western Eyes. L, 1911. TP: no *Colonial Library* ADS: dated *September, 1911*
Conrad, Joseph. Victory. L, 1915. TP: *36 ESSEX STREET, W.C.*
Conrad, Joseph. Youth. Edinburgh & L, 1902. ADS: dated *10/02*
Conroy, Pat. The Lords of Discipline. B, 1980.
  DJ: James Dickey review only
Constantine, K.C. The Rocksburg Railroad Murders. NY, 1972. DJ: No reviews on back
Cooper, James Fenimore. The Pathfinder. Ph, 1840.
  Vol I: copyright notice is absent
Coppard, A.E. Adam & Eve & Pinch Me. L, 1921.
  B: white buckram
Corso, Gregory. Bomb. SF, 1904. ADS: *Vestal Lady & Gasoline*
Corvo, Baron. The Desire and Pursuit of the Whole. L, 1934.
  B: dark green cloth
Corvo, Baron. In His Own Image. L, 1901. ADS: one leaf only
Cowley, Malcolm. F. Scott Fitzgerald: Tender is the Night . . . with the Author's Final Revisions. NY, 1951. CP: Scribner's seal xi.18: *xett* xiv.19: *tsandards* xviii.23: *b each* xviii.24: *accompanied*
Cozzens, James Gould. Confusion. B, 1924. B: pale grey-green cloth SP & FC: gilt stamping TE: red
Cozzens, James Gould. The Just and the Unjust. NY, (1942).
  CP: *Printed In The United States of America*
Cozzens, James Gould. S.S. San Pedro. NY, (1931).
  B: greyish green ST: silver
Crane, Hart. The Collected Poems of Hart Crane. NY, 1933.
  TP: *Inc* (no period)
Crane, Hart. The Letters of Hart Crane. NY, (1952).
  121: letter inverted
Crane, Hart. White Buildings. NY, 1926. TP: *Allan*
Crane, Stephen. The Collected Poems of Stephen Crane. NY, 1930. Running Head *The Black Riders* at top of left-hand page throughout book
Crane, Stephen. The Little Regiment. NY, 1896. PA: laid endpapers and flyleaves 197: *Gilbert Parker's Best Books* 202: concludes with *The Lilac Sunbonnet by S.R. Crockett*
Crane, Stephen. Maggie: A Girl of the Streets. (New York, 1893). TP: 11 lines of Roman type

Crane, Stephen. Men, Women and Boats. NY, (1921).
    69.19: missing word "*immediately*" after *almost*

Crane, Stephen. The Red Badge of Courage. NY, 1895.
    PA: laid with horizontal wire marks 225.last: *congratulated* perfect ADS: 3 works by Gilbert Parker; ADS end with *The Land of the Sun by Christian Reid*

Creeley, Robert. The Finger. Los Angeles, 1968. Wraps.
    13: no transposed lines

Creeley, Robert. The Island. NY, (1963). 145.20-22: out of order

Crews, Harry. Naked in Garden Hills. NY, 1969. B: medium to dark green cloth DJ: back: reviews of "*The Gospel Singer*"

Crichton, Michael. Jasper Johns. NY, (1977). 243: 3 errata listed DJ: rear panel: no barcode; rear flap: *8109-1161-2*

Cross, Amanda. In the Last Analysis. NY, (1964).
    CP: no usual *first printing* statement

Crumley, James. Dancing Bear. NY, (1983). BC: no square book club deboss DJ: front flap: price on flap

Cummings, E.E. The Enormous Room. NY, (1922).
    219.last: *shit* present or blacked out

Cummings, E.E. A Miscellany. NY, 1958. IL: (42) printed upright or tilting down to right but not a cancel

Dahlberg, Edward. Alms For Oblivion. Minneapolis, (1964). 53-54: integral

Dahlberg, Edward. Because I was Flesh. (Norfolk, Conn., 1964). PA: laid

Dahlberg, Edward. The Carnal Myth. NY, (1968).
    PA: light yellow laid

Dahlberg, Edward. The Leafless American. (Sausalito, 1967). 3-4: integral 27.18: period missing 97-8: integral

Daly, Thomas Augustine. Canzoni. Ph, 1906. 17: *feety*

Darwin, Charles. The Descent of Man, and Selection in Relation to Sex. L, 1871. ADS: *January 1, 1871* in both volumes CP: Volume II contains errata

Davenport, Guy. Flowers and Leaves. Highlands, N.C., 1966. B: dustjacket present, no spine label

Davenport, Guy. Pennant Key-Indexed Study Guide to Homer's Odyssey. Ph, (1967).
    B: white wrappers stamped in red, gilt and black

Page, Thomas Nelson. The Old Gentleman of the Black Stock. NY, 1897.
    Last P. text: *Merrymount Press* opposite

Page, Thomas Nelson. Red Rock. NY, 1898.
    FC: stamped in gilt, black & maroon CP: *Trow*

Page, Thomas Nelson. Two Little Confederates. NY, 1888. ADS: 10 pages at back

Parker, Dorothy. Death & Taxes. NY, 1931. CP: *Regular Edition Published June 1931 Second Printing Before Publication*

Patchen, Kenneth. The Love Poems of Kenneth Patchen. SF, (1960). WR: green and white Price: *75¢*

Paton, Alan. Cry, the Beloved Country. NY, 1948. DJ: rear flap perforated lower corner: book title & publisher

Percy, Walker. The Moviegoer. NY, 1961.
    CP: *First Edition* DJ: front flap: price and *0561* present

Perelman, S.J. Dawn Ginsbergh's Revenge. NY, (1929).
    B: apple-green plush

Petersen, Carl. Each in Its Ordered Place: A Faulkner Collector's Notebook. Ann Arbor, (1975).
    B: green morocco-grained cloth

Phillpotts, Eden. Children of the Mist. L, 1898.
    48: page # *8* present

Picasso, Pablo. Hunk of Skin. SF, (1968). B: sewn signatures 40: *Villiers Publications* notice
    No floral design on otherwise blank pages

Piercy, Marge. Fly Away Home. NY, (1984). DJ: front flap: *$16.95* DJ: back panel: *0284-1650* in serif, not "computer" typeface

Plante, David. The Ghost of Henry James. L, (1970).
    No glue stain or errata slip preceding front fly leaf

Ponicsan, Darryl. Cinderella Liberty. NY, (1973).
    DJ: front flap: *0573* Back panel: *SBN 06-013402-X*

Porter, Katherine Anne. Anniversary in a Country Cemetery. (NY, 1942).
    Price: *35¢* without rubber stamp cancel

Porter, Katherine Anne. The Collected Stories of Katherine Anne Porter. NY, (1965).
    DJ: back flap: *0262* not present

O'Connor, Flannery. A Good Man Is Hard to Find. NY, (1955). DJ: BC: *Wise Blood*

O'Hara, Frank. The Collected Poems of Frankk O'Hara. NY, 1971. DJ: Larry Rivers design

O'Hara, Frank. Second Avenue. NY, (1960). WR: grey & red printing CP: *Totem Press* address

O'Hara, John. Appointment In Samarra. NY, (1934). DP: erratum slip pasted on

O'Hara, John. The Ewings. NY, (1972). 231.16-17: error

O'Hara, John. Two By O'Hara. NY, (1979). CP: *B C D E* No usual Harcourt, Brace Jovanovich *first edition*

O'Neill, Eugene. Ah, Wilderness! L, (1934). DJ: no mention of Nobel prize

O'Neill, Eugene. Beyond the Horizon. NY, (1920). FC: capitals are 9/16" high

O'Neill, Eugene. The Emperor Jones, Diff'rent, The Straw. NY, (1921). B: *Eugene G. O'Neill*, plain unmottled boards

O'Neill, Eugene. Marco Millions. L, (1927). B: coated, sky blue V cloth SP: label present

O'Neill, Eugene. The Moon of the Caribbees, and Six Other Plays of the Sea. NY, 1919. Across top of covers: 7/8"

O'Neill, Eugene. The Provincetown Plays, Third Series. NY, 1916. WR: *Frank Shay, Publisher 1916*

O'Shaughnessy, Arthur W.E. Epic of Women. L, 1870. Pictorial title precedes title page

Oates, Joyce Carol. Them. NY, (1969). DJ: front flap: quote by Barbara Bannon DJ: back panel: *Photo: Robert Benyas*

Orwell, George. Animal Farm. NY, 1946. DJ: rear flap: lacks *Printed in U.S.A.*

Orwell, George. Animal Farm: A Fairy Story. L, 1945. DJ: Blue ad on back

Orwell, George. Nineteen Eighty-Four. NY, (1949). DJ: red BC: no book club deboss at lower corner near spine

Page, Thomas Nelson. Bred In the Bone. NY, 1904. B: green cloth

Page, Thomas Nelson. In Ole Virginia. NY, 1887. ADS: *Popular Books...Old Creole Days...*

Davenport, Guy. Pennant Key-Indexed Study Guide to Homer's Iliad. Ph, (1967). B: white wrappers stamped in red, gilt and black

Davidson, John. The Last Ballad. L, 1899. B: red buckram issue was suppressed; first published edition: blue buckram

Davidson, John. Miss Armstrong's and Other Circumstances. L, 1896. ADS: none at end

Davidson, John. New Ballads. L, 1897. ADS: dated *1896*

Davidson, John. Smith: A Tragedy. Glasgow, 1888. ADS: none

Davies, Robertson. Eros at Breakfast and Other Plays. T, 1949. PA: heavy textured B: dark crimson cloth

Davies, Robertson. Fifth Business. T, (1970). Table of Contents: 172 & 122 are reversed DJ: SP: no number at foot; no mention of book club selection (Note: Book Club edition has same error in Table of Contents.)

Davis, Richard Harding. Captain Macklin. NY, 1902. TE: gilt B: green cloth

Davis, Richard Harding. Cinderella and Other Stories. NY, 1896. FC: no picture of Cinderella

Davis, Richard Harding. Cuba In War Time. NY, 1897. 9: *Hearst* mentioned Last P. text: publisher's imprint

Davis, Richard Harding. The Cuban and Porto Rican Campaigns. NY, 1898. TP: *Gallagher*

Davis, Richard Harding. Gallegher and Other Stories. NY, 1891. P: wove ADS: no *Famous Women of the French Court*

Davis, Richard Harding. The King's Jackal. NY, 1898. HT: no list of author's works

Davis, Richard Harding. The Lion and the Unicorn. NY, 1899. B: cloth, not leather

Davis, Richard Harding. Our English Cousins. NY, 1894. ADS: *Van Bibber and Others* in cloth only *The Exiles and Other Stories* is without price

Davis, Richard Harding. Peace Manoeuvres. NY, 1914. TP: lines 6-7 of cautionary note: *manoeuvrs*

Davis, Richard Harding. Ranson's Folly. NY, 1902. 345: so numbered ADS: *Captain Macklin nearly ready*

Davis, Richard Harding. The Rulers of the Mediterranean. NY, 1894. ADS: none on CP

Davis, Richard Harding. Stories for Boys. NY, 1891.
    91: running head perfect
Davis, Richard Harding. Vanbibber and Others. NY, 1892.
    ADS: none at back
Davis, Richard Harding. Vera the Medium. NY, 1908.
    B: purple cloth
Davis, Richard Harding. The White Mice. NY, 1909.
    B: yellow cloth
Davis, Richard Harding. With Both Armies in South Africa. NY, 1900. IM: *Scribner's*
Davison, Lawrence H. *See* **Lawrence, D.H.**
De Camp, L. Sprague. Tales of Conan. NY, (1955).
    B: red paper boards ST: black on SP and FC
De La Mare, Walter. Come Hither. L, 1923. SP: blind rules
De La Mare, Walter. Dingdong Bell. L, 1924. ADS: 8 pages
De La Mare, Walter. Henry Brocken. L, 1904.
    TP: *[Walter Ramal* (no second bracket)
De La Mare, Walter. Memoirs of a Midget. L, 1921.
    CP: *Copyright 1921*
De La Mare, Walter. Rupert Brooke and the Intellectual Imagination. L, 1919. FC & SP: black stamping
De La Mare, Walter. The Three Mulla-Mulgars. L, 1910.
    Errata slip present TE: gilt BC: design in center
De Vries, Peter. Forever Panting. B, (1973). CP: *TO 5/73*
De Vries, Peter. Let Me Count the Ways. B, (1965).
    4.5-6up: lines are transposed
Deland, Margaret. The Awakening of Helena Richie. NY, 1906. DP: not boxed
Deland, Margaret. The Iron Woman. NY, 1911.
    TP: *Ezekiel* (no chapter and verse)
Deland, Margaret. Old Chester Tales. NY, 1899. 5.6 up: *Chelsea*
Derleth, August. Someone in the Dark. Sauk City, 1941.
    Height: 17.6 cm.
Dick, Philip. A Handful of Darkness. L, (1955).
    B: dark blue paper boards
Dickens, Charles. Oliver Twist. L, 1839.
    IL: "*Fireside*" plate and list of illustrations are absent

Nasby, Petroleum V. The Nasby Papers. Ind, 1864.
    FC: *Indianapolic*
Nathan, George Jean. A Book Without a Title. NY, 1918.
    IM: *Philip Goodman*
Nathan, George Jean. Mr. George Jean Nathan Presents. NY, 1917. B: black cloth ST: gilt
Nathan, Robert. Autumn. NY, 1921. B: light green
Nathan, Robert. Jonah. NY, 1925. B: green stamped
Nathan, Robert. Portrait of Jennie. NY, 1940. CP: *1939 and 1940* (2nd date often inked out)
    29.5: *Stuart* 171.14: *onght*
Nathan, Robert. Road of Ages. NY, 1935.
    CP: *1934* Col: paper by Warren
Nathan, Robert. There is Another Heaven. Ind, (1929).
    CP: integral & without *First Edition*
Newton, A. Edward. The Amenities of Book Collecting and Kindred Affections. B, 1918. 268: erratum slip present
    268.3: 9th word from left: *Piccadilly* DJ: no printing on covers, only on spine No index
Newton, A. Edward. This Book Collecting Game. B, 1928.
    49.running head: *Childhood*
Newton, Edward A. The Greatest Book in the World and Other Papers. B, (1925). List of Illustrations has *The Autograph of Cruikshank* on *341*
Nin, Anais. Cities of the Interior. (n.p., 1959).
    TP: no white label added 796: no ad facing
Nin, Anais. Realism and Reality. Yonkers, 1946. WR: purple
Nordhoff, Charles B. and Hall, James Norman. Mutiny on the Bounty. B, 1932. EP: plain
Norris, Frank. A Man's Woman. NY, 1900. B: light red cloth, decorative stamping SP: publisher's name
Norris, Frank. McTeague. NY, 1899. 106.last: *moment*
Norris, Frank. The Octopus. NY, 1901.
    All signature numbers present
Norris, Frank. The Responsibilities of the Novelist. NY, 1903. E: untrimmed
O'Cathasaigh, P. (Sean O'Casey). The Story of the Irish Citizen Army. Dublin, 1919. WR: grey

Morley, Christopher. **Shandygaff.** GC,1918. B:dark blue ST: gilt
Morley, Christopher. **Songs for a Little House.** NY, (1917).
  TP: Southwell quote facing
Morley, Christopher. **Travels in Philadelphia.** Ph, (1920).
  202.13: *along*
Morris, Wright. **Cause for Wonder.** NY, 1963.
  50 & 119 transposed
Morris, Wright. **The Field of Vision.** NY, (1956).
  DJ: black & blue printing
Morris, Wright. **God's Country and My People.** NY, (1958).
  DJ: *$7.95*
Mulford, Clarence. **Bar-20.** NY, 1907. List of illus.: *Blazing Star*
Mumie, Nolie. **Poker Alice.** Denver, 1951.
  MAP: New Mexico labeled *Nevada*
Murdoch, Iris. **The Red and the Green.** NY, (1965). E: clean cut B: halfbound black cloth over spine, black paper over boards
Murdoch, Iris. **Sartre Romantic Rationalist.** Cambridge, (1953). B: red cloth over boards DJ: *6s* price
Nabokoff, Vladimir. **Laughter in the Dark.** Ind, (1938).
  B: green cloth
Nabokov, Vladimir. **Despair.** NY, (1966).
  DJ: front flap: title in reddish-pink
Nabokov, Vladimir. **The Eye.** NY, (1965). CP: publisher's address present DJ: back flap: *Trident Press* DJ printed on white laid uncoated paper
Nabokov, Vladimir. **The Gift.** NY,(1963). B: 3.3cm wide DJ: *$5.95*
Nabokov, Vladimir. **Lolita.** NY, (1955). DJ: front panel: no statement *Complete Unexpurgated Edition*
Nabokov, Vladimir. **Lolita.** Paris, (1955). BC: *900 francs*
Nabokov, Vladimir. **Pale Fire.** NY, (1962). DJ: *First Impression*
Nabokov, Vladimir. **The Real Life of Sebastian Knight.** Norfolk, Conn., (1941). B: rough cloth, paper labels
Nabokov, Vladimir. **Speak, Memory a Memoir.** L, 1951.
  B: blue green cloth ST: black
  DJ: no "*Daily Mail*" device on SP or bottom front flap
Nabokov, Vladimir. **Three Russian Poets.** Norfolk, Ct., (1944). B: plain grey paper boards DJ: grey with brown lettering and *$1.00* in upper corner of front flap

Dickens, Charles. **The Personal History of David Copperfield.** L, 1850. TP: *1850*
Dickey, James. **Deliverance.** B, 1970. DJ: back flap: *6-84530*
Didion, Joan. **Play as It Lays.** NY, (1970).
  DJ: front flap: No SBN number
Dobie, J. Frank. **Coronado's Children.** Dallas, 1930.
  DP: *clean* absent
Dobie, J. Frank. **A Vaquero of the Brush Country.** Dallas, 1929. EP: maps say *Rio Grande River*
Doctorow, E.L. **Ragtime.** NY, (1975). DJ: back flap: no reviews
Doctorow, E.L. **The Waterworks.** NY, (1984). B: cloth over boards PA: uncut edges DJ: front cover: raised lettering DJ: back cover: *52300* in ISBN block
Doolittle, Hilda. **Collected Poems.** NY, 1925.
  191: *epigraph, tea* 214.7: *foul*
Doolittle, Hilda. **H.D.** NY, (1926). C: *Price 25 cents* absent
Donleavy, J.P. **The Ginger Man.** Paris, (1955). BC: *1500 francs*
Dos Passos, John. **The Garbage Man.** NY, (1926). B: chocolate brown boards, paper labels on FC and SP TE: trimmed
Dos Passos, John. **Manhattan Transfer.** NY, (1925).
  9: running headband: *p* perfect in *Ferryship* 298: *2* perfect in folio 328.22: *i* in *telling* broken
Dos Passos, John. **One Man's Initiation-1917.** L, (1920).
  35.32: *flat* broken & *d* obliterated Same error in 1st American edition, N.Y., 1922
Dos Passos, John. **Orient Express.** NY, (1927). B: lavender boards & lavender paper label SP: shiny blue cloth
Dos Passos, John. **Three Soldiers.** NY, (1921). B: 3 blank integral leaves at front, not including EPs EP: front & rear CP: no usual Doran *GHD* monogram 213.7up: *signing* DJ: publisher's blurb on front, spine and back
Douglas, Norman. **Alone.** L, 1921.
  140: postscript 156: erratum slip pasted in
Douglas, Norman. **D.H. Lawrence and Maurice Magnus.** Privately printed, n.p., 1924. TP: *1924* 9.8up: *9 May*
Douglas, Norman. **Fountains in the Sand.** L, 1912. B: blue c cloth blocked in white FC: gilt designs in upper left & right corners & gilt panelling IL: 16 plates

Douglas, Norman. Old Calabria. L, 1915.
    EP: white, no maps   ADS: 16 pages at end
Douglas, Norman. South Wind. L, (1917).
    335:1-2: lines transposed
Douglas, Norman. They Went. L, 1920. B: red cloth
Dowson, Ernest, *trans.* **Balzac. A Fille Aux Yeux d'Or.**
    B: gold cloth
Doyle, Arthur Conan. The Adventures of Sherlock Holmes.
    L, 1892. FC: street sign blank
Doyle, Arthur Conan. The Exploits of Brigadier Gerard.
    L, 1896. ADS: *30.11.95* or *10.2.96*
Doyle, Arthur Conan. The Great Shadow. NY, 1893.
    ADS: begin with Howell's *"The Coast of Bohemia"*
Doyle, Arthur Conan. The Hound of the Baskervilles. NY,
    (1902). FF: CP: no publication date
Doyle, Arthur Conan. The Mystery of Cloomber. L, 1889.
    ADS: [I] *Rowland's Kalydor, Aspinall's Enamel*; [II] *Ward and Downey's Cheap Novels, etc.;* [III] *Ward and Downey's Two-Shilling Novels*
Doyle, Arthur Conan. The Refugees. L, 1893. 3 vols.
    A one volume edition, also 1893, is second edition
Doyle, Arthur Conan. The Refugees. NY, 1893. TP: *1893*
Doyle, Arthur Conan. Rodney Stone. L, 1896. B: blue cloth
    TP: *London 1896* (not *London and Bombay*)
Doyle, Arthur Conan. The Sign of Four. L, 1890.
    SP: *Spencer Blackett's Standard Library*
Doyle, Arthur Conan. A Study in Scarlet. L, 1888. TP: *&*
    present Preface: *younger* ADS: last entry numbered *733*
Dreiser, Theodore. An American Tragedy. NY, 1925.
    2 vols. TP: *Boni & Liveright*
Dreiser, Theodore. The Financier. NY, 1912.
    B: blue mottled cloth
Dreiser, Theodore. Free and Other Stories. NY, 1918.
    TP: *B-L* monogram
Dreiser, Theodore. The "Genius." NY, 1915.
    497: so numbered   Book 1 3/4" across top of covers
Dreiser, Theodore. The Hand of the Potter. NY, 1918.
    Backstrip: natural linen   HT: tipped in and with ads on back   191: *it*   209: *several speeches*

Moore, George. Hail and Farewell. L, 1911-1912-(14).
    Salve: errata slip before P.1;
    Vale: HT: *III Ave* on back
Moore, George. The Lake. L, 1905. CP: New York copyright notice above London notice
Moore, George. A Modern Lover Volume II. L, 1883.
    B: putty-colored cloth   161-239: on proof paper
Moore, Marianne. Puss in Boots, The Sleeping Beauty & Cinderella. NY, 1963. B: blue calico
    C: *Macmillan Master Library Edition*
Morley, Christopher. Chimneysmoke. NY, (1921). Size: 6" x 9"
Morley, Christopher. Christopher Morley's Briefcase.
    Ph, 1936. 64: *PLAza*
Morley, Christopher. The Haunted Bookshop. NY, 1919.
    76: page so numbered; *Burroughs* in last line perfect
    100.1: *Sty*   163.1: *footfalls*
Morley, Christopher. Hide and Seek. NY, (1920). 41.2: *damsel*
Morley, Christopher. Hostages to Fortune. Haverford, 1925. TP: no double rule border
Morley, Christopher. Human Being. NY, 1932. DJ: front panel: copy under publisher's monogram ends with word *both* DJ: rear flap: quote by William Lyon Phelps under *THE BOOKS OF CHRISTOPHER MORLEY.*
    DJ: back panel: headed *On Being Abreast of Life*
Morley, Christopher. John Mistletoe. GC, 1931. 199: *23*
Morley, Christopher. Mince Pie. NY, (1919). vii.last: *of*
Morley, Christopher. Parnassus on Wheels. GC, 1917.
    4.8: *Y ears*
Morley, Christopher. Parsons' Pleasure. NY, (1923).
    Cover labels: *Parson's*
Morley, Christopher. Plum Pudding. NY, 1921. CP: *First Edition* (An exception to Doubleday Page which used *"First Edition"* beginning in 1922. This 1921 usage is likely from December, 1921 and the first book to use it.)
Morley, Christopher. The Rocking Horse. NY, (1919).
    TP: Burns quote facing
Morley, Christopher. Seacoast of Bohemia. GC, 1929.
    20.19: *raerly*

Millay, Edna St. Vincent. Renascence. NY, 1917. Trade edition. PA: watermarked *Glaslan* HT: 2 blank leaves preceding 1.3: *another* 8.8: *underground* 27.10: *a while*

Millay, Edna St. Vincent. Second April. NY, 1921. PA: watermarked *Glaslan*

Miller, Arthur. Death of a Salesman. NY, 1949. B: orange-red cloth CP: *Published by ... in March 1949*; no "W" present BC: no book club deboss at lower corner near spine

Miller, Arthur. A View from the Bridge. NY, 1955. TP: *1955* CP: Viking logotype present; no photograph credit given

Miller, Henry. Big Sur and the Oranges of Hieronymus Bosch. NY, 1957. DJ: no second printing statement

Miller, Henry. The Books in My Life. NY, (1952). TP: two leaves following four photos tipped-in

Miller, Henry. Four Visions of America. Santa Barbara, (1977). WR: entirely black

Miller, Henry. Letters to Anais Nin. NY, (1965). B: rough black cloth ST: gilt TE: stained red

Miller, Henry. Tropic of Cancer. Paris, (1934). CP: *First published September 1934* Wraparound band present

Miller, Henry. Tropic of Capricorn. Paris, (1939). SP: *prie* Errata slip inside

Miller, Joaquin. Songs of the Sierras. B, 1871. SP: *R.B.* at foot

Milne, A.A. When We Were Very Young. L, (1924). B: pictorial blue cloth EP: plain ix: not numbered

Mitchell, Donald Grant. About Old Story-Tellers: Of How and When They Lived, and What Stories They Told. NY, 1878. IM: *Rand, Avery & Co.*

Mitchell, Donald Grant. Rural Studies with Hints for Country Places. NY, 1867. Preface: last page is *iv*

Mitchell, Margaret. Gone With the Wind. NY, 1936. CP: *May, 1936* DJ: back panel: this title well down list of 17 titles

Mitchell, S. Weir. Hugh Wynne: Free Quaker. NY, 1897. E: all trimmed FC: red stamped designs Vol.I, 54.last: *in* Vol. II, 260.16: *. . . before us, . . .*

Moore, George. The Brook Kerith. Edinburgh, 1916. B: half brown imitation leather

Moore, George. Flowers of Passion. n.p., 1878. CP: *1877* Errata slip present

Dreiser, Theodore. A Hoosier Holiday. NY, 1916. SP: olive grey buckram 173.29: *ordinarily. The war! The war! They were chasing*

Dreiser, Theodore. Jennie Gerhardt. NY, 1911. SP: Author's name in full 22.30: *is*

Dreiser, Theodore. The Lost Phoebe and Old Rogaum and His Theresa. Girard, Kan., (1924). FC: author's name all capitals

Dreiser, Theodore. My Brother Paul, and W.L.S. Girard, Kan., (1924). FC: author's name all capitals

Dreiser, Theodore. Plays of the Natural and the Supernatural. NY, 1916. 228: next page is EP only

Dreiser, Theodore. Sister Carrie. NY, 1900. B: red buckram, black stamping EP: laid antique

Dreiser, Theodore. The Titan. NY, 1914. B: blue mottled cloth

Dreiser, Theodore. Tragic America. NY, (1931). 49.14: *filched* 100.13: *fraudulent* 130.4: *corruption* 130.5: *corrupted* 138.4up: *pirates* 380.4 up: *pirates*

Drinkwater, John. Abraham Lincoln. L, 1918. 5: hand-corrected misprint

Drinkwater, John. Cophetua. L, 1911. No errata slips at pages 6, 15, 16

Drinkwater, John. Lyric. L, (1916). PA: thick, chain lined paper

Drinkwater, John. The Old Legend, etc. n.p., 1913. B: green wrappers, dated *July 10, 1913.*

Drinkwater, John. Poems of Men and Hours. L, 1911. B: cream colored boards

Drinkwater, John. Rebellion. L, (1914). *First Edition* so stated

Drury, Allen. Advise and Consent. NY, 1959. DJ: front panel and spine: title and author's name in serif type

Duncan, Robert. Selected Poems. SF, (1959). B: saddle-stitched IBC: *Villiers Publications* Notice 62: *Venus of Lespuges begins*

Dunsany, Lord. A Dreamer's Tales. L, 1910. SP: *George Allen & Sons*

Dunsany, Lord. The Gods of Pegana. L, 1905. FC: drummer blind stamped

Dunsany, Lord. Plays of Gods and Men. Dublin, 1917. TP: The Talbot Press

Dunsany, Lord. Tales of Three Hemispheres. L, 1920.
  TP: *Printed in U.S.A.* printed with rubber stamp
Dunsany, Lord. Time and the Gods. L, 1906.
  B: brown boards, green backstrip
Durrell, Lawrence. The Black Book. NY, 1960. DJ: front flap:
  "*Lawrence Durrell's Black Book* ..." (not "*T.S. Eliot Said,* ...)
Durrell, Lawrence. Justine. NY, 1957. DJ: front flap: no review
  by Gerald Sykes Back Flap, last word: *Argentina* Back
  Panel: 5 reviews, 1st by John Betjeman Front Panel: 2
  reviews, by Cyril Connolly and Gore Vidal
Earle, Ferdinand. The Lyric Year. NY, 1912.
  25.13: *careful gentlemen*
Eco, Umberto. The Name of the Rose. NY, (1983).
  BC: no Book Club deboss at lower corner near spine
Eddison, E.R. The Worm Ouroboros. L, (1922).
  BC: Windmill blindstamped
Eddy, Mary Baker. *See* **Glover, Mary Baker.**
Edmonds, Walter D. Drums Along the Mohawk. B, 1936.
  DJ: Stefan Salter wraparound painting
Eliot, T.S. Anabasis. L, 1930. B: blue green cloth
  TE: green DJ: white, printed in green, red & black
Eliot, T.S. The Classics and the Man of Letters. L, 1942.
  TP: line 6: *the* with clear *t* (later *t* almost invisible)
Eliot, T.S. The Cocktail Party. NY, (1950). CP: no usual *first
  edition* statement & no bracketed code letters/numbers
Eliot, T.S. The Cocktail Party. L, (1950). 29.1: *here*
Eliot, T.S. The Confidential Clerk. L, (1954).
  7.2up: *Ihad* DJ: *10s6d*
Eliot, T.S. Dante. L, (1929). DJ: front flap, back panel: no reviews
Eliot, T.S. Elizabethan Essays. L, (1934). HT: *No. 21*
Eliot, T.S. The Film of Murder in the Cathedral. L, (1952).
  B: mauve cloth SP: stamped in blue and silver
Eliot, T.S. Four Quartets. NY, (1943). CP: *first American edition*
  DJ: front flap: *$2.00* & 20 lines of text;
  back panel: nine titles; back flap: blank
Eliot, T.S. Geoffrey Faber 1889-1961. L, (1961).
  B: brown paper boards
Eliot, T.S. Little Gidding. L, (1942). B: sewn, not wire-stitched

Mencken, H.L. In Defense of Women. NY, 1918. TP: *Ppilip*
Mencken, H.L. Europe After 8:15. NY, 1914.
  B: yellow cloth with gilt & blue stamping
Mencken, H.L. Man Verses the Man. NY, 1910.
  B: vertical ribbed red cloth ST: gilt
Mencken, H.L. The Philosophy of Friedrich Nietzsche.
  B, 1908. SP: *Friedrich* absent
Merrill, James. The Yellow Pages / 59 Poems. St. Louis,
  1971. B: pale yellow cover sheets FC: *The Yellow Pages*
Merritt, Abraham. The Ship of Ishtar. NY, 1926.
  B: red-brown cloth ST: yellow
Merton, Thomas. Bread in the Wilderness. (Norfolk,
  Conn., 1953). 24.running head: *BREAD IN THE
  WILDERNESS* inverted 30.25: *imagination which is no
  longer able to cope with immaterial* repeated at 30.27
  30.26: *and which is incapable of the simplest efforts to link
  two terms of* repeated at 30.28
  DJ: back flap: line 20: *anaology*
Merton, Thomas. Exile Ends in Glory. Milwaukee, (1948).
  DJ: back panel: Paragraph 3.3: *Griswald*
  Paragraph 8.3: *His talent for beyond*
Merton, Thomas. The Seven Storey Mountain. NY, (1948).
  DJ: BC: (*The author is second from the left*)
  B: off-white cloth w/black type; 35cm x 208cm
Michener, James. The Bridges at Toko-Ri. NY, (1953).
  No usual statement of First Edition
Michener, James. The Eagle and the Raven. Austin, (1990).
  EP: no accent mark on *Yucatan*
Michener, James. The Source. NY, (1965).
  CP: *First Printing* DJ: *$7.95*
Millar, Margaret. Wives and Lovers. NY, (1954). FF: DJ: lower
  front flap Book Club edition stated; if clipped, beware
Millay, Edna St.Vincent. Fatal Interview. NY,1931. TE: yellow
Millay, Edna St.Vincent. A Few Figs from Thistles. NY,
  (1922). TP: publisher's seal separates last 3 lines of type
Millay, Edna St.Vincent. The Lamp and the Bell. NY, 1921.
  WR: bright blue-green paper

McCutcheon, George Barr. Castle Craneycrow. C, 1902.
    B: green cloth   ST: green, yellow, white
McCutcheon, George Barr. Cowardice Court. NY, 1906.
    SP: *Coward/Ice*   EP: decorated
McCutcheon, George Barr. The Day of the Dog. NY, 1904.
    CP: *cave canum*
McCutcheon, George Barr. Graustark. C, 1901. 150.6: *Noble's*
McCutcheon, George Barr. Mr. Bingle. NY, 1915.
    SP: *Dodd, Mead & Co.*
McElroy, Joseph. Lookout Cartridge. NY, 1974.
    B: paper covered boards   SP: cloth
McFee, William. Aliens. L, 1914.   ADS: dated *1915*
McFee, William. Captain Macedoine's Daughter. GC, 1920.
    B: blue cloth   ST: yellow   SP: scroll-flourish design
McFee, William. Casuals of the Sea. L, 1916. SP: *Martin Secker*
    ADS: 16 pages at end, 1st and 3rd pages dated *MCMXVI*
McFee, William. Command. GC, 1922. 185.31: *though thim*
McFee, William. An Engineer's Notebook. NY, 1921.
    DJ: front: *By William McFee*
McFee, William. The Gates of the Caribbean. (n.p., 1922).
    BC: *Printed in the U.S.A.* not present
    Map: no dotted sailing route
McFee, William. Letters From an Ocean Tramp. L, 1908.
    SP: *Cassell & Co.*
McFee, William. Pilgrims of Adversity. GC, 1928.
    43.last: type perfect
McFee, William. A Port Said Miscellany. B, (1918).
    BC: list of seven titles
McMurtry, Larry. Daughters of the Tejas. Greenwich, 1965.   DJ: tan or grey paper earlier than white
McMurtry, Larry. In a Narrow Grave. Austin, 1968.
    105.12: *skycrappers*
McPhee, John. Basin and Range. NY, (1981).
    CP: no usual first printing statement
McPhee, John. Giving Good Weight. NY, (1979).
    BC: no book club deboss at lower corner near spine
Mencken, H.L. The Artist. B, 1912. Size: 6" x 4 1/2"
    B: grey & brown mottled boards

Eliot, T.S. Milton. L, 1947.
    20: *Printed in Great Britain at the University Press Oxford...*
Eliot, T.S. Notes Towards the Definition of Culture. NY, (1949). DJ: back panel: *Books by T.S. Eliot* lists 10 items
Eliot, T.S. Notes Towards the Definition of Culture. L, (1948). SP: *a*
Eliot, T.S. Poems. Richmond, 1919. 13.6: *aestival*   13.12: *capitaux*
Eliot, T.S. Poems 1909-1925. NY and C, (1932). EP: laid PA: watermarked *ANTIQUE DE LUXE BCMSH*
    DJ: cream, printed in blue; back flap: no price
Eliot, T.S. The Sacred Wood. L, (1920). SP: publisher's name 3 mm tall   ADS: absent   DJ: no subtitle on front
Eliot, T.S. The Waste Land. NY, 1922. B: flexible 41: *Mountain* not misspelled   Limitation numbers: 5 mm tall
Eliot, T.S. The Waste Land. Richmond, England, 1923.
    Label: asterisk border
Emerson, Ralph Waldo. Concord Centennial Discourse.
    Concord, 1835. B: [1]/4 2/4 [3]/4 4-6/4 7/2
Emerson, Ralph Waldo. The Conduct of Life. B, 1860.
    B: *Emerson's / Writings / Conduct / of / Life*
Emerson, Ralph Waldo. Letters and Social Aims. L, 1877.
    B: brown-orange S cloth   SP: *5* present   EP: pale yellow
Emerson, Ralph Waldo. Nature. B, 1836. 94: misnumbered *92*
Emerson, Ralph Waldo. Nature; An Essay and Lectures on the Times. L, 1844.   WR: Printed in colors, by Gregory & Collins   Contents Page: *Prospects* listed on p.56
    IM: no imprint on 138
Emerson, Ralph Waldo. Poems. L, 1847.
    FC: blindstamped, intersecting triple-rule frame
Evans, E. Everett. Man of Many Minds. Reading, (1955).
    B: blue cloth
Everson, William. X War Elegies. Waldport, 1943.
    B: black and yellow lettered wrappers
Farrell, James T. Judgment Day. NY, 1935.
    218.3: *thay*   378.15: *Shries*   414.22: *buged*
Farrell, James T. The Young Manhood of Studs Lonigan.
    NY, (1934). 88.18: *Connolly*   94.3 up: *Connolly*   199.21: *quies*   201.10: *... adore Thee!*   Errata slip present

Faulkner, William. Absalom, Absalom. NY, 1936.
    CP: no usual first edition statement
Faulkner, William. As I Lay Dying. NY, (1930).
    11: Initial *I* not aligned with text TE: brown
Faulkner, William. Collected Stories. NY, (1951).
    TE: blue TP: blue ink SP: *The* BC: no book club deboss at lower corner near spine
Faulkner, William. A Fable. NY, (1954).
    B: maroon cloth TE: grey
Faulkner, William. The Faulkner Reader. NY, (1954).
    BC: no book club deboss at lower corner near spine
Faulkner, William. Go Down, Moses. NY, (1942).
    B: black cloth TE: red
Faulkner, William. The Hamlet. NY, 1940.
    DJ: BC: ads for other Random House titles
Faulkner, William. Knight's Gambit. NY, (1949).
    CP: no usual first edition statement
Faulkner, William. Light in August. NY, (1932). B: coarse tan cloth ST: orange on FC; blue and orange on SP
Faulkner, William. The Mansion. NY, (1959). DJ: flap: *10 59*
Faulkner, William. Mosquitoes. L, 1964. B: grey-brown imitation cloth paperboards with vertical and horizontal pattern
Faulkner, William. Pylon. L, 1935. B: rose-brown TE: stained rose; bottom edge untrimmed ADS: 2 leaves at end
Faulkner, William. The Reivers. NY, (1962).
    BC: no square blind stamp at bottom
Faulkner, William. Requiem for a Nun. NY, (1951).
    B: pale green cloth TE: stained dark grey
    CP: no usual First Printing statement
    DJ: artist identified as *M. McKnight Kauffer*
Faulkner, William. Salmagundi. Milwaukee, 1932.
    E: bottom untrimmed
Faulkner, William. Sanctuary. NY, (1931).
    EP: grey with magenta design
Faulkner, William. Sanctuary. L, 1931.
    B: wine-red cloth ST: gilt ADS: 4 pages
Faulkner, William. Sartoris. L, 1932. B: blue cloth TE: blue

Maugham, W. Somerset. Of Human Bondage. NY, (1915).
    257.4: misprint present
Maugham, W. Somerset. Orientations. L, 1899.
    TE: gilt TP: in two colors and 243mm x 115mm
Maugham, W. Somerset. The Painted Veil. L, (1925).
    TP: cancelled Text with references to Hong-Kong, Happy Valley and The Peak throughout
Maugham, W. Somerset. The Sacred Flame. NY, 1928.
    Size: 6 3/4" x 5 1/16"
Maugham, W. Somerset. Theatre. L, 1937. 7-8: not on a stub
Maugham, W. Somerset. A Writer's Notebook. L, (1949).
    DJ: *Maughamiana* listed
Maxwell, William. The Chateau. NY, 1961. DJ: back panel: photo of author taken by Alfred A. Knopf
Maxwell, William. They Came Like Swallows. NY, 1937.
    DJ: BC: *1188*
McCarthy, Cormac. All the Pretty Horses. NY, 1992.
    DJ: no "Publishers Weekly" blurb; first letter on front flap not in color
McClure, J.B. Edison and His Inventions. C, 1879. ADS: no review of this title TP: *With copious illustrations* in one line (Includes *Uncle Remus and the Phonograph* by **Joel Chandler Harris**)
McClure, S.S. *See* **Cather, Willa.**
McCullers, Carson. The Ballad of the Sad Cafe/ The Novels and Stories of Carson McCullers. B, 1951.
    B: orange boards, red stamping DJ: front flap: *$5.00*
    DJ: rear panel: *373* & *104* not present
McCullers, Carson. The Member of the Wedding: A Play. (NY, 1951). B: brown stamping CP: no *New Directions* slug DJ: price present FP: photographic
McCullers, Carson. The Mortgaged Heart. B, 1971.
    B: 3-piece binding in two shades of rose cloth
McCullers, Carson. Reflections in a Golden Eye. (B), 1941.
    DJ: square cellophane window in front panel; paper is matte-finish
McCutcheon, George Barr. Beverly of Graustark. NY, 1904.
    TP: *HARRIS N FISHER*

Masters, Edgar Lee. A Book of Verses. C, 1898. B: grey
Masters, Edgar Lee. Mitch Miller. NY, 1920. Height : 7 3/4"
Masters, Edgar Lee. The New Spoon River. NY, (1924).
    CP: *Second Edition*
Masters, Edgar Lee. Spoon River Anthology. NY, 1915.
    Across top of covers: 7/8"
Maugham, W. Somerset. Cakes and Ale. L, (1930).
    147.14: *wone*
Maugham, W. Somerset. Cosmopolitans. GC, 1936. DJ: front panel: type is inside red-orange area; back flap: ad for *Don Fernando*; back panel: list headed *A Representative Collection of the books of W. Somerset Maugham* (Later DJ: green front panel, back panel ad for *Selected Short stories of Sinclair Lewis*, back flap: photo of Sinclair Lewis)
Maugham, W. Somerset. Cosmopolitans. L, 1936.
    5-6: cancel on a stub
Maugham, W. Somerset. Here and There. L, 1948. CP: *Reprint Society* B: greenish blue buckram with yellow label
Maugham, W. Somerset. The Land of Promise. L, 1913.
    TP: *Bickers & Son*
Maugham, W. Somerset. The Land of the Blessed Virgin. L, 1905. SP: lettering heights as follows: *The Land* 35mm, *of the* 24mm, *Blessed* 32mm, *Virgin* 23mm
Maugham, W. Somerset. The Making of a Saint. B, 1898.
    ADS: *In Press* under this title
Maugham, W. Somerset. The Merry Go Round. L, 1904.
    B: dark blue cloth Blank leaf at end
Maugham, W. Somerset. The Moon and Sixpence. L, 1919. ADS: 4 pages, integral; DeMorgan's work not listed as *posthumous*; 6 novels by Phillpotts listed; last listing *Jennie the Carter (ready shortly)*: page 4: *The Madhouse*
Maugham, W. Somerset. The Moon and Sixpence. NY, (1919). FC & SP: *Maughan*
Maugham, W. Somerset. Mrs. Craddock. L, 1902.
    B: dark green cloth TP: *Heinemann*
Maugham, W. Somerset. My South Sea Island. C, 1936.
    TP: *Sommerset*
Maugham, W. Somerset. Of Human Bondage. L, (1915).
    ADS: 1 page before HT and 16 pages at end

Faulkner, William. The Sound and the Fury. NY, (1929).
    DJ: no price; back cover: *Humanity Uprooted* priced *$3.00*
Faulkner, William. The Sound and the Fury. L, 1931.
    B: black cloth TE: stained red
Faulkner, William. The Town. NY, (1957). Trade Edition.
    B: red cloth TE: grey EP: grey patterned 327.8 & 10 repeated (corrected in orange binding copies with plain endpapers) DJ: front flap: *$3.95* and *5/57* at bottom
Faulkner, William. The Wild Palms. NY, (1939).
    SP: gilt stamped
Feibleman, Peter. Eating Together. B, (1984). CP: no date
Ferber, Edna. Come and Get It. GC, 1935. 403.5 up: *Byes*
Field, Eugene. The Love Affairs of a Bibliomaniac. NY, 1896.
    Opposite fly title, last entry: *Love Songs of Childhood*
Fisher, Vardis. In Tragic Life. Caldwell, ID, 1932.
    Doubleday Doran issue is second
Fisher, Vardis. No Villain Need Be. Caldwell, ID, 1936.
    Doubleday Doran issue is second
Fisher, Vardis. Passions Spin the Plot. Caldwell, ID, 1933.
    Doubleday Doran issue is second
Fisher, Vardis. We Are Betrayed. Caldwell, ID, (1935).
    Doubleday Doran issue is second
Fitzgerald, F. Scott. All the Sad Young Men. NY, 1926.
    CP: Scribner's seal   248: type perfect
    DJ: woman's lips on front unbattered
Fitzgerald, F. Scott. The Beautiful and Damned. NY, 1922.
    CP: Scribner's seal absent
    DJ: book title on front in white outlined in black
Fitzgerald, F. Scott. The Crack-Up. (n.p.), (1945).
    TP: red-brown and black   348: *Col*
Fitzgerald, F. Scott. The Great Gatsby. NY, 1925.
    DJ: back blurb, line 14: *jay Gatsby* 60.16: *chatter* 119.22: *northern* 165.16: *it's* 165.29: *away* 205.9-10: *sick in tired* 211.7-8: *Union Street station*
Fitzgerald, F. Scott. The Price was High. L/Melbourne/NY, (1979). 177: duplicates 162
Fitzgerald, F. Scott. The Stories of F. Scott Fitzgerald. NY, 1951. SP: *Malcom*

Fitzgerald, F. Scott. Taps at Reveille. NY, 1935. 349-352: not cancelled 351.29-30: *Oh, catch it - oh, catch it..*

Fitzgerald, F. Scott. Tender Is the Night. NY, 1951. CP: Scribner seal and 1948/51 dates, but no "*A*" xi.18: *xett* xiv.19: *tsandards* xviii.23: *b each* xviii.24: *accompanied*

Fitzgerald, F. Scott. Tender Is the Night. NY, 1934. DJ: front flap: blurbs by Eliot, Mencken and Rosenfeld

Flecker, James Elroy. The King of Alzander. L, 1914. B: scarlet buckram

Flecker, James Elroy. The Old Ships. L, n.d. B: blue-grey wrappers FC: ship, with mermaid present

Fleming, Ian. Chitty-Chitty-Bang-Bang. NY, (1964). B: red cloth ST: gold EP: pictorial DJ: back cover: *A Random House Book* DJ: price $3.50 CP: 6 line entry and 21 line dedication including PS

Fleming, Ian. The Spy Who Loved Me. L, (1962). TP: line between *e* and *m* in *Fleming*

Fleming, Ian. Thunderball. L, (1961). B: blind stamped boards

Ford, Ford Madox. The Inheritors. L, 1901. DP: none SP: *W & H* at sides of windmill in publisher's device; *HEINEMAN*

Ford, Ford Madox. The Inheritors. NY, 1901. DP: *To Boys and Christina*

Ford, Paul Leicester. The Great K. & A. Train Robbery. NY, 1897. Height: 7 1/4" TE: gilt, other edges untrimmed

Ford, Paul Leicester. The Honorable Peter Stirling and What People Thought of Him. NY, 1894. SP & FC: *Sterling*

Ford, Paul Leicester. Janice Meredith. NY, 1899. TP: dot over *N* in *Revolution* 121.22: *leader*

Forester, C.S. The Barbary Pirates. NY, (1953). B: red cloth DJ: back cover: ads present

Forester, C.S. Death to the French. L, (1932). SP: no Bodley's Head logo

Forester, C.S. The Indomitable Hornblower. B, (n.d. [1963]). CP: *A* present but no statement of printing or edition

Forester, C.S. Loves Lies Dreaming. Ind, (1927). FC: *C.E. Forester*

Malamud, Bernard. Dubin's Lives. NY, (1979). 231: bottom: *Why he asked her why,*

Malamud, Bernard. The Natural. NY, (1952). B: red or blue cloth preferred over grey

Malamud, Bernard. The Tenants. NY, (1971). B: orange cloth

Mansfield, Katherine. Bliss and Other Stories. L, 1920. DJ: white with author portrait 13: *3*

Mansfield, Katherine. The Doves' Nest and Other Stories. L, 1923. TP: back blank

Mansfield, Katherine. The Garden Party and Other Stories. L, (1922). 103.last: *sposition*

Mansfield, Katherine. In a German Pension. L, (1911). DJ: orange

Mansfield, Katherine. Letters To John Middleton Murray 1913-1922. L, 1951. 375-376 integral

Mansfield, Katherine. Prelude. Richmond, (1918). WR: design by J.D. Fergusson on front and back

Mansfield, Katherine. Something Childish and Other Stories. L, (1924). CP: *First published 1924* not present

Markham, Edwin. The Man with the Hoe and Other Poems. NY, 1899. 35.5: *fruitless*

Marquand, John P. The Late George Apley. B, 1937. 19.1: *Pretty Pearl*

Marquis, Don. The Dark Hours. NY, 1924. DJ: printed in black and yellow with type only on all printed surfaces

Marquis, Thomas B. A Warrior Who Fought Custer. Minneapolis, 1931. SP: *Midwest*

Masefield, John. Ballads and Poems. L, 1910. HT: two preceding blank leaves absent PA: laid with watermark

Masefield, John. A Book of Discoveries. B: yellow cloth TE: gilt

Masefield, John. The Faithful. L, (1915). EP: decorated

Masefield, John. Gallipoli. L, 1916. B: blue-grey cloth

Masefield, John. Jim Davis. L, (1911). FC & SP: gilt stamping TE: gilt

Masefield, John. Salt Water Ballads. L, 1902. TP: *Grant Richards*

Masefield, John. Sonnets of Good Cheer. (L, 1926). BC: *Copyright in Great Britain & U.S.A. By John Masefield*

Longfellow, Henry Wadsworth. Tales of a Wayside Inn.
L, 1864. v: *A Day in June* listed as at 239
242.verse 1: *Till at length it is or seems*

Longfellow, Henry Wadsworth. Voices of the Night.
Cambridge, 1839. (v): Prelude listed at *v* 18.10: *flowers a part* 23.11: *rose and fell,* 78.10: *His, Hector's arm*

Loos, Anita. "Gentlemen Prefer Blondes." NY, 1925.
Contents P.: *Divine*

Lowell, James Russell. Under the Willows and Other Poems. B, 1869. 286: erratum slip present

Lowell, James Russell. A Year's Life. B, 1841.
182: erratum slip present

Lucas, E.V. Over Bemerton's. L, 1908. 60.9: *barminess*

Ludlum, Robert. The Osterman Weekend. NY, (1972).
DJ: printed acetate; priced *$6.95* with *A 3918* at bottom right corner of BC

Lytle, Andrew. Bedford Forrest and His Critter Company. NY, 1931. Publisher not Putnam's

Macdonald, Ross. The Goodbye Look. NY, 1969. DJ: front panel: no quote by William Goldman "*The finest series...*"

MacFall, Haldane. The Wooings of Jezabel Pettyfer.
L, 1898. FC: picture of Jezabel

Machen, Arthur. The Angels of Mons. The Bowmen and Other Legends of the War. L, 1915. B: blue boards with medieval warrior on front cover

Machen, Arthur. The Hill of Dreams. L, 1907.
SP: *E. Grant Richards*

Mailer, Norman. Cannibals and Christians. NY, 1966.
FP: color photograph of Vertical City tipped in

Mailer, Norman. The Prisoner of Sex. B/T, (1971).
DJ: front flap: *$5.95*

Mailer, Norman. The White Negro. SF, 1957. FC: *35 cents*

Mailer, Norman. Why Are We In Vietnam. NY, (1967).
DP: integral with *Farbar*

Major, Charles. When Knighthood was In Flower.
Ind, 1898. TP: no author's name   TP: *1897*

Malamud, Bernard. The Assistant. NY, (1957).
DJ: back panel: reviews of *The Natural*

Forester, C.S. Marionettes at Home. L, (1936).
DJ: SP: no *3/6 net*

Forester, C.S. Napoleon and His Court. L, (1924). B: green-blue cloth ADS: dated *324* at rear FC: gilt stamped

Forester, C.S. The Sky and the Forest. L, (1948).
210.last: full stop at end of line   DJ: *s* in *Forest* damaged

Forester, C.S. The Voyage of the Annie Marble. L, (1929).
SP: no Bodley's Head logo

Forester, C.S. Victor Emmanuel II. L, (1927). B: blue

Forster, E.M. Abinger Harvest. L, 1936.
278-281: *A Flood in the Office*

Forster, E.M. Desmond MacCarthy. (n.p.), 1952. FC: *Foster*

Forster, E.M. The Eternal Moment. L, 1928. SP: gilt stamping

Forster, E.M. Howard's End. L, 1910. [348]: *A Stepson of the Soil*

Forster, E.M. Howard's End. NY, 1910. B: 424 pages

Forster, E. M. Where Angels Fear to Tread. Edinburgh, 1905. ADS: no mention of this title

Fowles, John. The Collector. L, (1963). DJ: front flap: no blurbs

Fowles, John. The Tree. (L, 1979). DJ: back flap: *Magnus*

Fox, Jr. John William. Crittenden, A Kentucky Story of Love and War. NY, 1900. B: red cloth SP: stamped *Crittenden A Kentucky Story of Love & War By John Fox Jr. Scribners.*

Fox, Jr. John William. A Cumberland Vendetta. NY, 1896.
Table of contents: last entry *Hell for Sartain*

Fox, Jr. John William. The Heart of the Hills. NY, 1913.
[ii]: *Postage Extra* in the listing *The Heart of the Hills*

Fox, Jr. John William. A Knight of the Cumberland. NY, 1906. FC: stamped in black and gilt

Fox, Jr. John William. The Little Shepherd of Kingdom Come. NY, 1903. HT: no ads on verso 61.14: *laugh*

Fox, Jr. John William. The Trail of the Lonesome Pine. NY, 1908. CP: Scribner's seal   DP: *F.S.* 3/16" high

Francis, Dick. Bonecrack. NY, (1972). Last page: *72 ...3 2 1*

Francis, Dick. Enquiry. NY, (1969). CP: *First Edition*
Last Page: *23456789*

Francis, Dick. Knockdown. NY, (1974). BC: no book club deboss at lower corner near spine

Francis, Dick. Odds Against. NY, (1966).
    DJ: front flap: 3 reviews not present
Francis, Dick. Rat Race. NY, (1971).
    Last blank page: *71 72 73 74 10 9 8 7 6 5 4 3 2 1*
Francis, Dick. Slay-Ride. NY, (1974).
    Last page: *...76 77 10 9 8 7 6 5 4 3 2 1*
Francis, Dick. Smokescreen. NY, (1973).
    Last page: *... 76 77 10 9 8 7 6 5 4 3 2 1*
Fraser, Antonia. Your Royal Hostage. NY, 1988.
    123:6 *Pompey* not present 123:7 *from* not present
Frederick, Harold. Seth's Brother's Wife. NY, 1887.
    CP: *1886* ADS: absent
Freeman, Mary Wilkins. Pembroke. NY, 1894.
    ADS: No reviews of this book
Frost, Robert. A Boy's Will. L, 1913.
    B: pebbled bronze cloth E: all trimmed
Frost, Robert. A Boy's Will. NY, 1915.
    B: blue fine linen cloth EP: white 14.last: *Aind*
Frost, Robert. Collected Poems. NY, (1930). IM: *Holt* 128: *laces*
Frost, Robert. The Gold Hesperidee. (Cortland), (1935).
    Col: *Cortland NY/A* 7.2up: *Twas Sunday and Square Hale was dressed for meeting.*
Frost, Robert. In the Clearing. NY, (1962).
    DJ: back panel: black type on white background
Frost, Robert. Mountain Interval. NY, (1916).
    88: verses 6&7 duplicate 93.6 up: *Come*
Frost, Robert. North of Boston. L, (1914).
    B: coarse green cloth measuring 195 x 154mm
    L: gilt FC: blind rule border all around
Frost, Robert. North of Boston. NY, 1915.
    TP: tipped-in on stub, other sheets English
Frost, Robert. The Poetry of Robert Frost. NY, (1969).
    BC: no square deboss at lower corner near spine
    DJ: front flap: *$10.95*; *1169* at bottom of text
    DJ: PA: heavy stock, laminated; not thin, dull stock
Frost, Robert. West Running Brook. NY, 1928.
    Limited edition: 44: *roams* CP: *First edition* absent
    Trade edition: 44: *roams* CP: *First edition* absent

London, Jack. Revolution. C, (1909).
    Front WR: union seal & *284*
London, Jack. Revolution and Other Essays. NY, 1910.
    B: dark red cloth
London, Jack. The Scab. C, (1905). TP: *56 5th Ave., Chicago*
London, Jack. Scorn of Women. NY, 1906. SP: white
London, Jack. The Son of the Wolf. B, 1900.
    B: slate black ST: silver 8 preliminary pages are unnumbered Flyleaf at back
London, Jack. Stories of Ships and the Sea. Girard, KS, (1922). CP: *1922*
London, Jack. The Strength of the Strong. C, 1911.
    ADS: *Kinzie Street*
London, Jack. Theft. NY, 1910. SP: white 47.1: *that* 65.1: *perplexed*
London, Jack. The Tramp. NY, (1904). TP: *125 E. 2304 St, NY*
London, Jack. White Fang. NY, 1906. TP: integral
Longfellow, Henry Wadsworth. Aftermath. L, 1873.
    64.verse 7: *Little cared for his Babes* B: green cloth
Longfellow, Henry Wadsworth. Evangeline, a Tale of Acadia. B, 1847. 61.1: *Long*
Longfellow, Henry Wadsworth. The Golden Legend. L, 1851.
    145: misnumbered *541* 241: signature mark *R* is present
    242.1: of a truth
Longfellow, Henry Wadsworth. The Golden Legend. B, 1851.
    IM: *MDCCCLI*
Longfellow, Henry Wadsworth. In the Harbor Ultima Thule - Part II: B, 1882. 27.2up: *I can longer* Leaf (2)6 not cancel
Longfellow, Henry Wadsworth. Kavanagh, a Tale. B, 1849.
    25.12: *Cartwright's* 96.14: *Arian* 177.11: *hte*
Longfellow, Henry Wadsworth. Keramos and Other Poems.
    B, 1878. SP: *Houghton, Osgood & Co.*
Longfellow, Henry Wadsworth. Masque of Pandora and Other Poems. L, 1875. SP: *James R. Osgood & Co*
Longfellow, Henry Wadsworth. The Song of Hiawatha. B, 1855. 32.11: *In the moon* 39.11: *Wahonomin* 96.7: *Dove*
Longfellow, Henry Wadsworth. Tales of a Wayside Inn. B, 1863. ADS: page 11 *Tales of a Wayside Inn* is unpriced and described as *nearly ready*

Lewis, Alfred Henry. Richard Croker. NY, 1901.
    26.last paragraph: transposed lines
Lewis, Alfred Henry. Wolfville. NY, (1897). 19.18: *Moore* perfect
Lewis, Janet. Poems 1924-44. Denver, (1950).
    B: green cloth   L: gilt
Lewis, Sinclair. Arrowsmith. NY, (1925).
    1st trade ed. CP: *Second Printing January, 1925*
Lewis, Sinclair. Babbitt. NY, (1922). 49.4: *Purdy* 49.5: *my fellow*
Lewis, Sinclair. Cheap and Contented Labor. NY, 1929.
    TP: no quotation marks before *Dodsworth*
Lewis, Sinclair. Elmer Gantry. NY, (1927). SP: *G* looks like a *C*
Lewis, Sinclair. Main Street. NY, 1920. 49: page number perfect   54: page number perfect   387.42: *may* perfect
Lewis, Sinclair writing as **Graham, Tom. Hike and the Aeroplane.** NY, (1912). CP: *August 1912*
Lincoln, Joseph C. Mr. Pratt. NY, 1906.
    Table of Contents: all page numbers missing
Lindbergh, Anne Morrow. North To the Orient. NY, 1935.
    11: *Abacadabra*
Lindbergh, Charles A. We. NY, 1927. DJ: front flap: copy begins *They called me "Lucky," but luck isn't enough..*
London, Jack. The Abysmal Brute. NY, 1913.
    ST: yellow and black/deep green
London, Jack. The Acorn-Planter. NY, 1916. SP: white
London, Jack. Burning Daylight. NY, 1910.
    SP: *The/MacMillan/Company*   ADS: blank leaf follows
London, Jack. The Call of the Wild. NY, 1903.
    B: vertically ribbed cloth
London, Jack. The Cruise of the Dazzler. NY, 1902.
    CP: *Published October, 1902*
London, Jack. The Dream of Debs. C, n.d.
    BC: ad for book by Gustavus Myers
London, Jack. The Game. NY, 1905.
    CP: Metropolitan magazine rubber stamp absent
London, Jack. Hearts of Three. NY, 1920.
    CP: *Published London, 1918.*
London, Jack. John Barleycorn. NY, 1913.
    343: one blank leaf following

Gaddis, William. JR. L, (1976).
    DJ: front flap: *condom* not crossed out
Galsworthy, John. The Burning Spear. L, 1919.
    TP: author's name not present   ADS: 32 pages
Galsworthy, John. Captures. L, 1923. (ii): list of *New Fiction*
Galsworthy, John. The Country House. L, 1907.
    BC: windmill device lower right
Galsworthy, John. In Chancery. L, 1920.
    B: bright green cloth
Galsworthy, John. The Dark Flower. L, 1913.
    B: dark red cloth   ADS: 7 pages front, 16 pages back
Galsworthy, John. The Forsyte Saga. L, 1922.
    Genealogical table pulls out to right
Galsworthy, John. The Freelands. L, (1915).
    B: green cloth, gilt stamping
Galsworthy, John. The Full Moon. L, 1915.
    Back leaf: no cast list
Galsworthy, John. The Island Pharisees. L, 1904.
    Publisher's list: this title absent; *Wolf Wyllarde* present
Galsworthy, John. The Little Dream. L, (1911).   No inserted note: *Certain small alterations have been made for the acting version of this play.*
Galsworthy, John. The Man of Property. L, 1906. Three divisional half-titles inserted P.1, text: signature mark present   200: bar of music broken   375.6: *24*
Galsworthy, John. Plays Vol. II. The Eldest Son, The Little Dream, Justice. L, 1912. ADS: present at end
Galsworthy, John. A Sheaf. L, 1916.
    B: dark brown boards   TE: brown
Galsworthy, John. The Silver Box, Joy, Strife. L, 1910.
    List of the cast: *Halland; Holmwood; Pilling; O'Mally.*
    BC: publisher's device at center
Galsworthy, John. The Silver Spoon. L, (1926).
    DJ: printed in silver and green on black background
Galsworthy, John. Swan Song. L, 1928. 44.10: *Thn eobtained*
Galsworthy, John. Verses New and Old. L, 1926.
    FP: portrait of author, head and shoulders only

Galsworthy, John. Villa Rubein. L, 1900. B: Cherry-colored cloth SP: publisher's name in plain stamping

Galsworthy, John *writing as* **Sinjohn, John. Jocelyn.** L, 1898. 257.3 up: *you*

Galsworthy, John *writing as* **Sinjohn, John. A Man of Devon.** Edinburgh & L, 1901. ADS: *4/01*

Garcia Marquez, Gabriel. The Autumn of the Patriarch. NY, (1976). CP: *First Edition*, row of numbers ends with *5*

Garcia Marquez, Gabriel. Chronicle of a Death Foretold. NY, 1983. DJ: front flap: *One Hundred Days of Solitude*

Garcia Marquez, Gabriel. In Evil Hour. NY, (1979). DJ: spine: *Marquez*, not *Garcia Marquez*

Garcia Marquez, Gabriel. One Hundred Years of Solitude. NY, (1970). CP: *First Edition* Last Leaf: no row of numbers DJ: front flap: *!* at end of first paragraph

Gardner, John. The Liquidator. NY, (1964). DJ: price present

Gardner, John. Nickel Mountain. NY, 1973. DJ: rear flap: *12/73*

Garland, Hamlin. Main-Travelled Roads. B, 1891. Across pages: 9/16"

Gilbert, William S. The Pirates of Penzance. L, 1880. 11.12: *True piece of mind*

Ginsberg, Allen. The Fall of America: Poems of These States, 1965-1971. SF, (1972). C: white w/black type

Ginsberg, Allen. Kaddish and Other Poems, 1958-1960. SF, (1961). BC: 10-line publisher's statement 100: *Villiers Publications* notice B: sewn signatures

Ginsberg, Allen. Planet News, 1961-1967. SF, (1968). IBC: *Villiers Publications* notice B: sewn signatures NOTE: Perfect-bound copies with *First-American Edition: November, 1968* on copyright page are 2nd printing

Ginsberg, Allen. Reality Sandwiches, 1953-1960. SF, (1963). CP: line 5: *t* in *Pocket* is lower than other letters

Gissing, George. Eve's Ransom. ADS: 16 pp. at end *Autumn Season, 1894.*

Gissing, George. The Private Papers of Henry Ryecroft. Westminster, 1903. ADS: 3 leaves

Gissing, George. The Town Traveller. L, 1898. ADS: *September 1898*

Gissing, George. Vernailda. L, 1904. ADS: 16 pages at end

Lawrence, D.H. The Lost Girl. L, (1920.) 268:15: *whether she noticed anything in the bedrooms, in the beds* 256-258: not tipped in

Lawrence, D.H. Love Poems and Others. L, 1913. xiv.16: *is* ("*i*" is intact)

Lawrence, D.H. The Prussian Officer and Other Stories. L, (1914). B: dark blue cloth boards ADS: 20 pages

Lawrence, D.H. The Rainbow. L, 1915. ADS: *Autumn, 1914*

Lawrence, D.H. Sons and Lovers. L, (1913). TP: integral, no date

Lawrence, D.H. The Trespassers. L, 1912. ADS: 20 pages

Lawrence, D.H. The White Peacock. L, 1911. B: Heinemann windmill blindstamped on lower cover 227-230: integral

Lawrence, D.H. The White Peacock. NY, 1910. TP: 1910 and not tipped in 227-30 tipped in BC: publisher's blind stamped windmill device

Lawrence, D.H. Women in Love. L, (1921). 63.19: *girl with dark, soft, fluffy hair* 61.31: *come round to the flat and see*

Lawrence, D.H., *writing as* **Lawrence H. Davison. Movements in European History.** L, 1921. B: brown cloth

Lawrence, T.E. The Letters of T.E. Lawrence. L/T, (1938). 495: letter signed *T.E.L.* 182.9: *Baltic*

Lawrence, T.E. Selected Letters of T.E. Lawrence. L, (1952). CP: *First Published 1938/reprinted 1952*

Leacock, Stephen. Mark Twain. NY, 1933. DJ: woodcut of Twain is 2 5/16"; back panel: this title last on list; second ink color orange

Least Heat Moon, William. Blue Highways. B, (1982). DJ: front flap, lower corner: *01831700* DJ: back flap: reviews by Mowatt and Dillard only

LeCarre, John. The Spy Who Came In From the Cold. NY, (1964). CP: no "*W*" DJ: priced at *$4.50*; back panel: 3 quotes, by Graham Greene, Alec Waugh & J.B. Priestley

Le Gallienne, Richard. Young Lives. Bristol, n.d. TP: *All rights reserved* at top

Leonard, Elmore. Valdez Is Coming. (NY, 1970). Price: *60 cents*

Levertov, Denise. The Double Image. L, 1946. TP: *Levertoff*

Kipling, Rudyard. Plain Tales From the Hills. Calcutta, 1888.
    B: olive green cloth   FC: picture of hills and plains
    ADS: *Dec. 1887*
Kipling, Rudyard. Plain Tales From the Hills. NY, (1890).
    Publisher: *Frank F. Lovell & Co.*   FC: *Kudyard*
    IM: *142-144 Worth St.*
Kipling, Rudyard. Schoolboy Lyrics. Lahore, 1881.   WR: blank
Kipling, Rudyard. Soldiers Three. Allahabad, 1888.
    CP: *Reprinted in chief from the Week's News.*
Kipling, Rudyard. The Story of the Gadsbys. Allahabad,
    n.d.   CP: *Reprinted in chief from the Week's News.*
Kipling, Rudyard. Wee Willie Winkle. Allahabad, n.d.
    FC: lower right corner *A.H.* with periods present
Knight, William Allen. The Song of Our Syrian Guest. B,
    1903. Next to last page: *The Love Watch* due early in 1904
Knowles, John. A Separate Peace. NY, 1960.   DJ: pictorial
Koestler, Arthur. Darkness At Noon. NY, 1941.
    CP: *First Printing*   (not merely *Set up and printed*)
Kosinski, Jerzy. The Painted Bird. B, 1965.
    270: extra line of type at top
Kosinski, Jerzy. The Painted Bird. B, 1976. 2nd ed.
    BC: no book club deboss at lower corner near spine
Lamb, Wally. She's Come Undone. NY, (1992).   DJ: front flap:
    price present; upper bar code *52100*
    DJ: rear panel: middle bar code *76714 02100*
**Lanier, Sidney. Florida: Its Scenery, Climate, and History,
    etc.** Ph, 1876.   CP: *1875*
**Lardner, Ring. Treat 'Em Rough: Letters From Jack the
    Kaiser Killer.** Ind, (1918). 6: no poem to R.W.L.
Lardner, Ring. What Of It. NY, 1925. pp. 200-201 transposed
Lathen, Emma. A Place For Murder. NY, (1963).
    CP: no usual statement of first printing
Lawrence, D.H. Amores: Poems. L, 1916. ADS: 16 pages
Lawrence, D.H. Cavalleria Rusticana and Other Stories.
    L, (1928). B: red cloth
Lawrence, D.H. Little Novels of Sicily. NY, 1925.
    B: red cloth   SP: yellow paper label printed in red

Gissing, George. Will Warburton. L, 1905. ADS: 16 pages at end
Glasgow, Ellen. The Ancient Law. NY, 1908.
    31.12: *hardly a ship*   216.5: *more that*   338.14: *in it*
Glasgow, Ellen. The Deliverance. NY, 1904.
    B: smooth red cloth   IL: only 3 present
    9.12: *negro*   18.22: *negroes*   21.7: *negress*
Glasgow, Ellen. The Descendant. NY, 1897.
    SP: author's name absent   IM: *New York* only
Glasgow, Ellen. Phases of an Inferior Planet. NY, 1898.
    At back: erratum slip re page 194
Glasgow, Ellen. The Voice of the People. NY, 1900.
    TP: publisher's seal   4.2-3: *the inalienable affability*
Glasgow, Ellen. The Wheel of Life. NY, 1906.
    267.7: *she should*   499.17: *forefeiture*
Glover, Mary Baker (Eddy). Science and Health. B, 1875.
    Errata slip without index
Goodman, Paul. Five Years. NY, 1966.
    DJ: blue, black & white printing
Goodman, Paul. Pieces of Three. (Harrington Park, N.J.,
    1942).   WR: cream
Goodman, Paul. Stop-Light. Harrington Park, N.J., 1941.
    DJ: all letters above illustrations are red
Gordon, Caroline. Aleck Maury, Sportsman. NY, 1934.
    B: green cloth
Gorey, Edward (Ogdred Weary). The Curious Sofa. NY,
    (1961). C: *$1.50*   (second printings may have evidence of
    glue where price sticker (*$1.75*) was removed
Gorey, Edward. The Epiplectic Bicycle. NY, (1969).   DJ: *$3.00*
Gorey, Edward. The Fatal Lozenge/ An Alphabet. NY,
    (1960). Front wrapper: *$1.25*
Gorey, Edward. The Object-Lesson. GC, 1958.
    B: white boards, beige and black pictorial stamping
Gorey, Edward. The Wuggly Ump. Ph/NY, (1963).
    CP: No usual Lippincott *first edition*
Gover, Robert. One Hundred Dollar Misunderstanding. NY,
    (1962). DJ: one color printing
Graham, Tom. *See* **Lewis, Sinclair.**

Grau, Shirley Ann. The Black Prince and Other Stories. NY, 1955. DJ: no reviews

Graves, Robert. Antigua, Penny, Puce. L, (1936). 100.11: *ytyle* 103.15: *being* 293: has lowered "*l*" as last letter

Graves, Robert. But It Still Goes On. L, (1930). 157: *the child s the bare* DJ: green printed in blue and black

Graves, Robert. Claudius the God. NY, 1935. B: dark blue cloth FC: blind stamped, not gilt DJ: *$3.00* below text, not in corner DJ: back flap: first word *suddenly*

Graves, Robert. Collected Poems. GC, 1961.
DJ: *C.P.* over price

Graves, Robert. Collected Poems 1955. GC, 1955.
TP: *1955* printed above the publisher's name

Graves, Robert. Collected Poems 1966. GC, 1966.
FC: painting by Robert Kipniss Cover price: *$1.75*

Graves, Robert. The English Ballad. L, 1927. B: bright red cloth; height: 19.5 cm DJ: height: 19.8 cm TE: only edge that is trimmed

Graves, Robert. Fairies and Fusiliers. L, (1917). B: orange-red B cloth ST: gilt SP: publisher's imprint 5/8" across

Graves, Robert. Good-Bye to All That. L, (1929).
341-343: Sassoon poem

Graves, Robert. Good-Bye to All That. NY, (1930). DJ: front flap: *$3.00*; DJ: BC: this title in ads which are printed in red and black; DJ: back flap: ad for "*The Paris Gun*" reads *Illustrated, $3.50*; DJ: FC: publisher's logo stamped in middle; double ruled lines run diagonally on FC and BC

Graves, Robert. I, Claudius. NY, 1934. B: dark slate-blue cloth FC: medallion blind stamped; no gold stamping SP: publisher's name, not emblem DJ: *$3.00*

Graves, Robert. John Skelton. L, (1927).
No errata 22: footnote 10: *can* with broken *c*

Graves, Robert. King Jesus. L, (1946). DJ: *12s.6d.net* front flap: text begins *A recent book by Robert Graves| [double rule] | The Golden Fleece* DJ: back flap: *Apt/G 416*

Graves, Robert. Lars Porsena. L, (1927). ADS: 15 pages bound in at rear with this title on p.12 under heading "*Nearly Ready*" DJ: back cover: this title listed 4th from bottom

King, Stephen. The Dark Tower: the Gunslinger. West Kingston, (1982). DJ: also lists limited edition price

King, Stephen. Cujo. NY, (1981). DJ: front flap: *$13.95* and no ISBN # or *09153581* present

King, Stephen. Four Past Midnight. NY, (1990).
FC: gilt embossed *S.K.*

King, Stephen. My Pretty Pony. (NY, 1988).
SP: red leather label with silver lettering

King, Stephen. Nightmares and Dreamscapes. L, 1993.
DJ: *15.99* (pounds) 448: *The House on Maple Street*

King, Stephen. Pet Sematary. GC, 1983. DJ: back cover: *1982* listed as date of *Caretakers by Tabitha King*

King, Stephen. Salem's Lot. GC, 1975.
DJ: *$8.95*; reference to *Father Cody* in write-up

King, Stephen. The Stand. GC, 1978. DJ: *$12.95*

Kipling, Rudyard. The Ballad of East and West. By Yussuf. NY, 1889 (1890).
Publisher's address: *86 Nassau St.*

Kipling, Rudyard. The Ballad of the King's Jest. By Yussuf. NY, 1890. Publisher's address: *86 Nassau St.*

Kipling, Rudyard. Departmental Ditties, Barrack-Room Ballads and Other Verses. NY, (1890).
TP: *150 Worth St.*

Kipling, Rudyard. Evarra and His Gods. NY, 1890.
Publisher's Address: *86 Nassau St.*

Kipling, Rudyard. From Sea To Sea. Letters of Travel. NY, 1899. 2 vols. Vol. II, 90.12: *fifteen feet* Vol. II, 153.26: *carcasses tacked round her*

Kipling, Rudyard. In Black and White. Allahabad, n.d.
CP: *Reprinted in chief from the Week's News*

Kipling, Rudyard. Kim. NY, 1901.
Rhymed chapter heads at Ch.8 and Ch.13 only

Kipling, Rudyard. The Light That Failed. L, 1891. ADS: 55 pp.

Kipling, Rudyard. Mine Own People. NY, (1891).
Publisher: *United States Book Co., 150 Worth St.*

Kipling, Rudyard. The Phantom Rickshaw and Other Tales. Allahabad, n.d. CP: *Reprinted in chief from the Week's News*

Kent, Rockwell. Wilderness: a Journal of Quiet Adventure in Alaska. NY, 1920. B: grey linen ST: gilt
Kent, Rockwell, (editor). **World Famous Paintings.** NY, 1939.
    FC: *The Laughing Cavalier*
Kerouac, Jack. Dharma Bums. (L, 1959). CP: *First Published 1950*, may or may not have label correcting this error
Kerouac, Jack. Lonesome Traveller. (L, 1962). B: very dark brown boards SP: gilt lettering
Kerouac, Jack. Maggie Cassidy. (L, 1960).
    FC: Maggie pictured as blond in long black stockings
Kerouac, Jack. Maggie Cassidy. NY, (1959). TP: 2 page spread
Kerouac, Jack. On the Road. (L, 1958).
    DJ: back flap: author's photo
Kerouac, Jack. The Scripture of the Golden Eternity. NY, (1960). B: white wraps printed in purple
Kerouac, Jack. The Subterraneans. (L, 1960).
    B: red, paper covered boards
Kerouac, Jack. The Subterraneans. NY, (1958).
    Grove Press. Cover: printing in all white
Kerouac, Jack. Vanity of Duluz. (L, 1969).
    B: green boards DJ: priced in shillings
Kerouac, Jack. Visions of Cody. NY, 1973.
    CP: *123456789BPBP798765432*
Kesey, Ken. Sometimes a Great Notion. NY, (1964).
    HT: *Viking* logo present
    DJ: Hank Krangler noted as photographer
Kilmer, Joyce. Literature in the Making. NY, (1917).
    B: brown cloth L: gilt
Kilmer, Joyce. Main Street and Other Poems. NY, (1917).
    B: brown boards TE: gilt
Kilmer, Joyce. Summer of Love. NY, 1911. SP: *Baker & Taylor*
Kilmer, Joyce. Trees and Other Poems. NY, (1914).
    B: grey boards, paper labels TE: gilt
    CP: *Printed in the United States of America* absent
King, Martin Luther. Strength To Love. NY, (1963).
    Size: 8 1/2" x 6" not 8 3/16" x 5 9/16"
King, Stephen. Danse Macabre. NY, (1981). CP: *RRD281*

Graves, Robert. Lawrence and the Arabs. L, (1927).
    B: mustard-orange cloth
Graves, Robert. Man Does, Woman Is. L, 1964.
    DJ: back cover: reviews of "*New Poems 1962*" on back
Graves, Robert. Mrs. Fisher. L, 1928. 4: Skelton quotation
Graves, Robert. On English Poetry. NY, 1922.
    B: orange paper over boards;
    leaves *93/94, 97/98, 125/126* & *133/134* are cancels
Graves, Robert. On English Poetry. L, 1922. B: yellow cloth with cobbled design on FC, but not SP
    DJ: BC: *LONDON: WILLIAM HEINEMANN*
Graves, Robert. Seven Days in New Crete. L, (1949).
    Contents Page: *page v* printed on page
Graves, Robert. The Siege and Fall of Troy. GC, [1963].
    DJ: back flap: no reviews of this book DJ: SP: publisher's name & emblem present DJ: front flap: *T.S.A.F.O.T. | UP TO 16 | PRICE, $3.50.*
Graves, Robert. T.E. Lawrence to His Biographer. GC, 1963.
    CP: *Johnathan* DJ: SP: orange, olive green and black
Graves, Robert. Two Wise Children. (NY, 1966). B: green cloth, covers blank SP: black lettering DJ: *$2.73 net*
Graves, Robert. The White Goddess. L, (1948).
    DJ: yellow paper printed in black & red DJ: front flap: no reviews; back flap: unprinted
Green, Anna Katherine. The Amethyst Box. Ind, (1905).
    CP: *April*
Green, Anna Katherine. The Filigree Ball. Ind, (1903).
    CP: *March* and printer's slug in red
Green, Anna Katherine. The House in the Mist. Ind, (1905).
    CP: *April*
Green, Anna Katherine. The Leavenworth Case. NY, 1878.
    215.last: *resh*
Green, Anna Katherine. The Millionaire Baby. Ind, (1905).
    CP: *January*
Greenaway, Kate. A Day in a Child's Life. L, 1881. B: decorated boards; no ring of roses with girls in center
Greenaway, Kate. Under the Window. L, (1878).
    14: *End of Contents* TP: printer's imprint present

Greene, Graham. A Sort of Life. L, (1971).
    177.4: *Sir John Barrie*
Greene, Graham. The Basement Room and Other Stories. L, (1935). B: green cloth
Greene, Graham. Dr. Fischer of Geneva or The Bomb Party. L, (1980). 9.4: *leave alone*
Greene, Graham. The End of the Affair. NY, 1951. DJ: back panel: Waugh comment doesn't have quote from Time
Greene, Graham. The Human Factor. L, (1978).
    TP: publisher's device
Greene, Graham. It's a Battlefield. L, (1934). DJ: price 7/6
Greene, Graham. The Labyrinthine Ways. NY, 1940.
    165: *A voice said...*
Greene, Graham. The Lawless Roads. L/NY/T, (1939).
    B: red cloth ST: gilt
Greene, Graham. Loser Takes All. L, (1955).
    DJ: blue and yellow with a cafe table on left turning into a roulette wheel on right
Greene, Graham. Travels With My Aunt. NY, 1970.
    BC: no book club deboss at lower corner near spine
Grey, Zane. NOTE: all his books from 1910 up are published by Harper's with the exception of *The Redheaded Outfield* by Grosset & Dunlap
Grey, Zane. Betty Zane. NY, (1903).
    TP: no mention of edition
Grey, Zane. The Border Legion. NY, (1916). CP: *E-Q*
Grey, Zane. Captives of the Desert. NY, 1952. CP: *B-B*
Grey, Zane. The Day of the Beast. NY, (1922). CP: *C-W*
Grey, Zane. The Deer Stalker. NY, (1925). CP: *D-Y*
    DJ: no "*Christian Herald*" announcement
Grey, Zane. Desert Gold. NY, 1913. CP: *C-N*
Grey, Zane. The Desert of Wheat. NY, (1919). CP: *A-T*
Grey, Zane. Ken Ward in the Jungle. NY, 1912. CP: *H-M*
Grey, Zane. The Last Trail. NY, (1909). ADS: 6 pages; 1st page starts *Abner Daniel*; 2nd page starts *The Circle*, 3rd page starts *The House on Cherry Street*; 4th page starts *Max*; 5th page starts *The Reconstructed Marriage*; 6th page starts *Susan Clegg* & ends with *The Younger Set*; 2 pages of ads listing *52-58 Duane Street* as Burt's address

James, Henry. Terminations. NY, 1895. B: pale green-on-white linen grain cloth SP: *Harper Brothers* ornament
James, Henry. Transatlantic Sketches. B, 1875.
    SP: *James R. Osgood and Company*
James, Henry. Travelling Companions. NY, 1919. B: pine green linen-grain cloth SP: *Liveright* measures 3/4" long
James, Henry. The Wheel of Time. NY, 1893.
    B: dark green linen-grain cloth TE: ochre stained
James, Will. Flint Spears. NY, 1938. CP: Scribner's *A* absent
Jarrell, Randall. The Animal Family. (NY, 1965).
    EP: tan, laid, uncoated, rough
Jarrell, Randall. The Animal Family. (NY, 1965).
    Library edition: SP: printed in red including publisher's name EP: white
Jeffers, Robinson. Medea. NY, 1946.
    99-100: integral 99.21: *least* absent
Jewett, Sarah Orne. Betty Leicester. B, 1890.
    TP: ads opposite end with this title
Jewett, Sarah Orne. Deephaven. B, 1877. 65.16: *was*
Jewett, Sarah Orne. Play Days: a Book of Stories For Children. B, 1878. B: blue silk cloth
Jewett, Sarah Orne. The Tory Lover. B and NY, 1901.
    278: *Lackynge, my love, I goe from place to place*
Jones, David. In Parenthesis. NY, (1961). Size: 8 1/2" tall
    Contents P: no introduction by Eliot TE: unstained
Jones, James. From Here To Eternity. NY, 1951.
    DJ: back panel: photo of author
Jones, LeRoi. Preface To a Twenty Volume Suicide Note . . . NY, (1961). TP: *32 West Eighth Street* CP: *Totem Press* Last P: ads fill page
Joyce, James. Chamber Music. L, 1907. EP: thick laid paper Signature "C" in book: poems well centered on pages
Kelly, Walt. Pogo. NY, (1951). TP: no date
Kemelman, Harry. Friday the Rabbi Slept Late. NY, 1964.
    DJ: front flap: *$3.95* (not *$4.95*) Bulk of book substantially more than those with *$4.95* dustjacket
Kent, Rockwell. Voyage Southward From the Straits of Magellan. NY, 1924. B: grey linen or tan buckram ST: decorative gilt

Ishiguro, Kazuo. An Artist of the Floating World. L, (1986).
CP: *Butler & Tanner*

James, Henry. The American Scene. L, 1907. B: burgundy red buckram FC: double-rule border in blind

James, Henry. The American Scene. NY, 1907.
B: cobalt blue vertical-ribbed cloth FC: gilt stamping

James, Henry. The Awkward Age. L, 1899.
ADS: last page *The Latest Fiction*

James, Henry. A Bundle of Letters. B, (1880). FC: *JR*,

James, Henry. Confidence. B, 1880.
SP: *Houghton, Osgood and Company*

James, Henry. Daisy Miller. NY, 1879. ADS: lists 79 titles only

James, Henry. Daisy Miller: a Comedy. B, 1883.
SP: *J.R. Osgood monogram*

James, Henry. English Hours. L, 1905. B: grey linen-grain cloth

James, Henry. Italian Hours. L, 1909.
BC: publisher's device blindstamped

James, Henry. Julia Bride. NY and L, 1909. B: claret fine-wave-grain cloth or maroon diagonal fine-ribbed cloth; serif-lettered publisher's imprint

James, Henry. The Novels and Tales of Henry James, NY edition. NY, 1907. B: smooth silky plum cloth

James, Henry. A Passionate Pilgrim. B, 1875.
SP: *James R. Osgood and Co.*

James, Henry. Picture and Text. NY, 1893.
B: dark green linen-grain cloth

James, Henry. The Portrait of a Lady. NY, 1882. (ii): full stop after imprint *Copyright, 1881* B: light tan or forest green

James, Henry. The Private Life. NY, 1893.
B: dark green linen-grain cloth TE: ochre-stained

James, Henry. Roderick Hudson. B, 1876. IM: *Osgood*

James, Henry. The Sacred Fount. NY, 1901.
B: smooth silky biscuit cloth

James, Henry. The Sense of the Past. NY, 1917.
B: dull olive-brown smooth sateen cloth

James, Henry. A Small Boy and Others. NY, 1913. ADS: 11 lines long; *Notes of a Son and Brother* absent

James, Henry. Tales of Three Cities. B, 1884. B: dull violet-brown, ochre or blue diagonal, fine-ribbed cloth

Grey, Zane. The Light of the Western Stars. NY, 1914.
CP: *M-N*

Grey, Zane. The Lone Star Ranger. NY, 1915. CP: *M-O*

Grey, Zane. The Man of the Forest. NY, (1920). CP: *A-U*

Grey, Zane. The Mysterious Rider. NY, (1921). CP: *I-U*

Grey, Zane. The Rainbow Trail. NY, (1915). CP: *F-P*

Grey, Zane. The Redheaded Outfield and Other Baseball Stories. NY, (1920). ADS: first page: 11 titles, last is *The Last of The Great Scouts* DJ: back panel: 18 titles excluding *Tales of Fishes* and *The Man of the Forest*

Grey, Zane. Rogue River Feud. NY, 1948. CP: *C-X*

Grey, Zane. Roping Lions in the Grand Canyon. NY, 1924.
CP: *B-Y*

Grey, Zane. The Spirit of the Border. NY, (1906). ADS: 4 pages; ads at back headed *Good Fiction worth reading*; 1st page begins *Colonial Free Lance*, 2nd page begins *Darnley*; 3rd page begins *Guy Fawkes*; 4th page begins *Winsor Castle*; 1st page lists 5 books, other pages no more than 3 books; Publisher's address: *52-58 Duane Street*

Grey, Zane. Stranger From the Tonto. NY, (1956). CP: *G-F*

Grey, Zane. Tales of Fishes. NY, (1919). CP: *F-T*

Grey, Zane. Tales of Lonely Trails. NY, (1922). CP: *G-W*

Grey, Zane. Tales of Southern Rivers. L, (1924). CP: *H-Y*

Grey, Zane. Tales of Southern Rivers. NY, (1924). CP: *H-Y*

Grey, Zane. To the Last Man. NY, (1922). CP: *K-V*

Grey, Zane. The U.P. Trail. NY, (1918). CP: *A-S*

Grey, Zane. Wildfire. NY, (1917). CP: *L-Q*

Grey, Zane. The Wolf Tracker. NY, 1930. CP: *C-E*

Grey, Zane. Zane Grey Omnibus. NY, 1943. CP: *B-S*

Grey, Zane. Zane Grey's Book of Camps & Trails. NY, 1931.
CP: *G-F*

Grile, Dod. See Bierce, Ambrose.

Grisham, John. Pelican Brief. NY, (1992). DJ: front flap: no ISBN bar code; back panel *9780385421980* and *52250*

Guiney, Louise Imogen. Songs at the Start. B, 1884.
110: errata slip inserted

Habberton, John. Helen's Babies. B, 1876. Size: 1 3/16"

Haggard, H. Rider. Allan Quatermain. L, 1887.
78: *Quartermain* 88: *Dongo Egere*

Haggard, H. Rider. Ayesha: The Return of She. L,
   1905. 49.32: *Khublighan*   207.21: *heirophant*
   BC: no ornaments
Haggard, H. Rider. King Solomon's Mines. L, 1885.
   10.14: *Bamamgwato*   122.27: *to let twins to live*
   ADS: dated *5G.8.85*
Haggard, H. Rider. She: A History of Adventure. L,
   1887. 59.22: *gentlemen*   88.4: *mysogynist*
   126.26: *had*   258.37: *it*   269.38: *Godness me*
Hall, Marguerite Radclyffe. The Well of Loneliness. Paris,
   1928. 50.3: *whip*
**Hardy, Thomas. The Dynasts: A Drama of the Napoleonic
   Wars.** L, 1903-06-08. (3 vols) Vol.I: TP: *1903*
Hardy, Thomas. Far From the Madding Crowd. L, 1874.
   2 vols. 2.1: *sacrament*
Hardy, Thomas. A Group of Noble Dames. (L, 1891).
   B: brown cloth, gilt design EP: yellow
**Hardy, Thomas. A Laodicean; or, the Castle of the de
   Stancys.** L, 1881. 3 vols. HT: *or* omitted
Hardy, Thomas. A Pair of Blue Eyes. L, 1873. 3 vols.
   Vol. II, 5.last: *louds* B: green cloth, gilt design
Hardy, Thomas. The Return of the Native. L, 1878. 3 vols.
   TP: *'A Pair of Blue Eyes*
Hardy, Thomas. Tess of the D'Urbervilles. (L, 1891).
   Chapter *XXV* for *XXXV* Vol. 3: 198: *road*
Harris, Joel Chandler. The Chronicles of Aunt Minervy Ann.
   NY, 1899. TE: gilt Edges: all trimmed PA: wove
Harris, Joel Chandler. On the Wings of Occasions. NY,
   1900. B: light green cloth ST: black only
   FC: wing & sword design
**Harris, Joel Chandler. Uncle Remus His Songs and His
   Sayings.** NY, 1881. 9.last line: *presumptive* (233): *New
   Books. A Treatise on the Practice of Medicine*
   ADS: no mention of this book
Harte, Bret. The Luck of Roaring Camp. B, 1870.
   Brown of Calaveras absent from text
Harte, Bret. A Millionaire of Rough-and-Ready. B, 1887.
   B: Pages total 299 only

**Howells, William Dean. Lives and Speeches of Abraham
   Lincoln and Hannibal Hamlin.** Columbus, OH, 1860.
   TP: *Columbus, O* (no period) 95-96: blank
Howells, William Dean. A Modern Instance. B, 1882.
   Across top of covers: 1 1/4"
Howells, William Dean. My Mark Twain. NY, 1907. TE: gilt
Howells, William Dean. The Rise of Silas Lapham. B, 1885.
   176.last: type perfect
   TP: facing ad: *Mr. Howell's Latest Works*
Howells, William Dean. Their Wedding Journey. B, 1872.
   TP: *& co.* (with period, next to last line)
Howells, William Dean. The Undiscovered Country. B, 1880.
   B: black floral stamp all over
Hudson, W.H. A Crystal Age. L,1887. TP: author's name absent
Hudson, W.H. Green Mansions. L, 1904.
   B: green cloth BC: no publisher's seal
Hudson, W.H. The Purple Land that England Lost. L, 1885.
   Vol. 2, ADS: *October*
Hughes, Langston. Freedom's Plow. NY, (1943).
   WR: *Buy United States War Bonds and Stamps*
Hughes, Langston. Jim Crow's Last Stand. (n.p. [Atlanta]),
   (1943). Contents Page: Belt upside down
Hughes, Langston. Simply Heavenly. (NY, 1959).
   Front Wrapper: 4th line: *Books*
Hughes, Langston. The Weary Blues. NY, 1926.
   DJ: no blurb for "*Fine Clothes to the Jew*"
Huneker, James. Franz Liszt. NY, 1911. B: silky cloth TE: gilt
Huneker, James. Iconoclasts. NY, 1905. CP: *Norwood Press*
Huneker, James. Old Fogy. Ph, (1913). EP: figured design
Huneker, James. Painted Veils. NY, 1920.
   WR: *Blandford Book U.S.A.*
Hurston, Zora Neale. Moses, Man of the Mountain. NY,
   (1939). B: reddish-brown cloth
Huxley, Aldous. Limbo. L, 1920. TE: brown
Huxley, Aldous. On the Margin. L, 1923. vi: numbered *v*
**Huxley, Aldous, (translator). A Virgin Heart by Remy de
   Gormont.** NY, 1921. 3: *V* at foot of page

Holmes, Oliver Wendell. Border Lines of Knowledge in Some Provinces of Medical Sciences. B, 1862.
SP: *Ticknor & Co.* imprint

Holmes, Oliver Wendell. Over the Teacups. B & NY, 1891.
ADS: *Over the Teacups* has no price; *Breakfast Table Series* described as *10 volumes at $17*

Holmes, Oliver Wendell. The Poet at the Breakfast-Table. B, 1872. 9.running head: *Talle*

Honig, Edwin. Spring Journal. Middletown, CT., (1968). Errata slip re: *Nativity* laid in Stanza 1, lines 2 & 3 are the same

Hough, Emerson. 54-40 or Fight. Ind, (1909). CP: *January*

Hough, Emerson. The King of Gee Whiz. Ind, 1906. 26.last word: *Banjo*

Hough, Emerson. The Law of the Land. Ind, (1904). CP: *October*

Hough, Emerson. The Mississippi Bubble. Ind, (1902). CP: *April* SP: *Hough* (no *Emerson*)

Hough, Emerson. The Story of the Outlaw. NY, 1907. v: rule at top

Hough, Emerson. The Way to the West. Ind, (1903). CP: *October*

Housman, A.E. Last Poems. L, 1922. 52: no comma after *love* and no semicolon after *rain*

Housman, A.E. A Shropshire Lad. L, 1896. Label: *Shropshire* is 33mm wide

Howe, E.W. Preaching from the Audience. Girard, KS. (1926). FC: *Candid Comments on Life*

Howe, E.W. The Story of a Country Town. Atchison, KS, 1882. B: green cloth EP: rubber stamped SP: no stamping at bottom IFC: *D. Caldwell, manufacturer. Atchison Kan*

Howe, E.W. Success Easier than Failure. Girard, KS, (1927). FC: no subtitle

Howe, E.W. When a Woman Enjoys Herself. Girard, KS, (1928). FC: *And Other Small Town Stories*

Howells, William Dean. Between the Dark and the Daylight. NY, 1907. B: green cloth ST: gilt

Howells, William Dean. A Boy's Town. NY, 1980. (iv): illustration present

Howells, William Dean. A Foregone Conclusion. B, 1875. TP: no ads opposite

Harte, Bret. Miss. An Idyl of Red Mountain. NY, (1873). TP: Harte's name present WR: Harte's name on front

Harte, Bret. Poems. B, 1871. TP: *Fields, Osgood* SP: *F O & Co.* 136: *S.T.K.*

Harte, Bret. Thankful Blossom. B, 1877. B: *James R. Osgood & Co.* monogram on front SP: *James R. Osgood &Co.* imprint

Harte, Bret. A Waif of the Plains. L, 1890. SP: *A Waif of the Plains &c.* ADS: *Oct 1889*

Hawkes, John. The Beetle Leg. (NY, 1951). B: light orange cloth

Hawkes, John. The Cannibal. (Norfolk, Ct., 1949). B: grey cloth

Hawkes, John. The Goose on the Grave. (NY, 1954). B: very shiny black boards DJ: no crossing out of price, no rubber stamped *$4.50*

Hawkes, John. The Lime Twig. (NY, 1961). SP: stamping runs down spine DJ: back panel: no ad for *Second Skin*

Heaney, Seamus. Eleven Poems. (Belfast, 1965). B: warm-white laid wrappers, red-violet (not dark maroon) sun-symbol

Hearn, Lafcadio. Japanese Lyrics. B, 1915. TP: inserted on stub No ad for *The new Poetry Series*

Hearn, Lafcadio. Kotto. NY, 1902. TP: background upside down w/artist's monogram upper right

Hearn, Lafcadio. Kwaidan. B, 1904. B: blue cloth

Hearn, Lafcadio, trans. Gautier. One of Cleopatra's Nights. NY, 1882. SP: *R. Worthington*

Hearn, Lafcadio. Out of the East. B, 1895. B: across top of covers: 1 5/16"

Hearn, Lafcadio. The Romance of the Milky Way. B, 1905. B: grey linen

Hearn, Lafcadio. Stray Leaves from Strange Literature. B, 1884. SP: *J.R. & O.*

Hearn, Lafcadio. Youma the Story of a West Indian Slave. NY, 1890. B: white calico with blue all-over design TE: trimmed, others untrimmed

Hecht, Ben. Erik Dorn. NY, 1921. B: plum cloth ST: yellow

Hecht, Ben. A Jew in Love. NY, 1931. 306.last: *Christ*

Hegan, Alice Caldwell (Alice Hegan Rice). Mrs. Wiggs of the Cabbage Patch. NY, 1901. FC: sky is gold

Heggen, Thomas. Mister Roberts. B, 1946. DJ: front flap: *$2.50*
Heinlein, Robert. Assignment in Eternity. Reading, PA, (1953). B: brick red cloth, gilt SP: *Heinlein* 3 mm high
Heinlein, Robert. The Cat Who Walks Through Walls. NY, (1985). 300.3: *Enterprise...*; erratum slip laid in
Heinlein, Robert. Methuselah's Children. Hicksville, NY, (1958). DJ: BC: 35 titles and *80 East 11th St, NY 3*
Heinlein, Robert. Orphans of the Sky. NY, (1964). BC: no book club deboss at lower corner near spine
Heller, Joseph. Catch-22. NY, 1961. DJ: back panel: no reviews
Hemingway, Ernest. Across the River and Into the Trees. NY, 1950. DJ: stamped in yellow 21.26: *papadopohi*
Hemingway, Ernest. A Farewell to Arms. L, (1929). 66.28: *seriosu*
Hemingway, Ernest. A Farewell to Arms. NY, 1929. (x): no disclaimer "*None of these characters...*" DJ: front flap: *Katharine Barclay*
Hemingway, Ernest. For Whom the Bell Tolls. NY, 1940. DJ: rear photo lacks photographer's name beneath
Hemingway, Ernest. The Hemingway Reader. NY, 1953. DJ: front flap: *$5.00* ; back flap: no *Printed in U.S.A.* & *005*
Hemingway, Ernest. In Our Time: Stories. NY, 1930. CP: publisher seal present
Hemingway, Ernest. Men Without Women. NY, 1927. PA: 80-pound B: weighs more than 15.8 oz. 3: perfect *3* DJ: tan with black lettering; no blurbs in three orange bands across front DJ: front flap: *$2.00*, otherwise blank; back flap and BC: blank
Hemingway, Ernest. Old Man and the Sea. NY, 1952. DJ: BC: photograph has deep blue ink; two lines of small production symbols appear at end of text FF: CP has *Kingsport Press* [Tennessee] imprint BC: no book club deboss at lower corner near spine
Hemingway, Ernest. The Spanish Earth. Cleveland, 1938. EP: pictorial showing F.A.I. banner
Hemingway, Ernest. The Sun Also Rises. NY, 1926. 181.26: *stoppped* DJ: *In Our Times* listed as prior title

Henry, O. Cabbages and Kings. NY, 1904. SP: *McClure, Phillips & Co.*
Henry, O. The Four Million. NY, 1906. SP: *McClure Phillips*
Henry, O. Let Me Feel Your Pulse. NY, 1910. CP: *October*
Henry, O. Postscripts. NY, 1923. B: red cloth ST: gilt
Henry, O. Roads of Destiny. NY, 1909. 9.6: *H* missing
Henry, O. The Voice of the City. NY, 1908. SP: *McClure*
Herford, Oliver. Pen and Inklings. NY, (1893). 21.18 of poem: *waived*
Hergesheimer, Joseph. Gold and Iron. NY, 1918. TE: black
Hergesheimer, Joseph. Linda London. NY, 1919. B: smooth blue cloth
Hergesheimer, Joseph. The Three Black Pennys. NY, 1917. Fly-TP: lower edge of medallion 2" from page bottom
Herman, William. *See* **Bierce, Ambrose.**
Hewlett, Maurice. A Masque of Dead Florentines. L, 1895. B: tan buckram
Hewlett, Maurice. Mrs. Lancelot. L, 1912. ADS: first 4 pages unnumbered
Hewlett, Maurice. Pan and the Young Shepherd. L, 1898. B: light green boards with picture of Pan on back cover
Heyward, DuBose. Porgy. NY, (1925). B: gilt stamping
Hillerman, Tony. The Great Taos Bank Robbery. Albuquerque, (1973). B: yellow-grey cloth DJ: back panel: single illustration EP: light yellow-brown
Hillerman, Tony. Listening Woman. NY, (1978). BC: no blindstamped square at bottom near spine
Hjorstberg, William. Falling Angel. NY, (1978). B: light olive paper over boards with red cloth spine DJ: gold foil ink DJ: back flap: *Printed in U.S.A.* absent Height: 8 5/8"
Hodgson, Ralph. The Last Blackbird and Other Lines. L, 1907. E: uncut
Holmes, Oliver Wendell. Astraea. B, 1850. B: glazed cream-yellow paper boards 33: signature mark is set under the *en* in *fragment*
Holmes, Oliver Wendell. Before the Curfew and Other Poems. B & NY, 1888. ADS: *Before the Curfew* is *$1.25*